Relationship Needs, Framework, and Models

I0178735

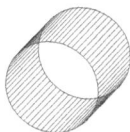

This Author's Books
(As at 2016)

<u>Non fiction</u>

The Nature of Love and Relationships 2011, **2016** 2nd Edition
Doubts and Decisions for Living:
  Volume I: The Foundation of Human Thoughts **2014**
  Volume II: The Sanctity of Human Spirit **2014**
  Volume III: The Structure of Human Life **2014**
Relationship Facts, Trends, and Choices **2016**
The Mysteries of Life, Love, and Happiness **2016**
Marriage and Divorce Hardships **2016**
Gender Qualities, Quirks, and Quarrels **2016**
Relationship Needs, Framework, and Models **2016**

<u>Fiction</u>

Persian Moons 2007, **2016** 2nd Edition
Midnight Gate-opener 2011, **2016** 2nd Edition
My Lousy Life Stories **2014**

Love and Relationships Series
Guidelines for Success

Relationship

Needs,

Framework, and

Models

Tom Omidi, Ph.D.

Love and Relationships Series # 5
Copyright © 2016 by Tom Omidi

All rights reserved. No part of this book may be repro-
duced, translated, or transmitted in any form or by any
means—graphic, electronic or mechanical, including pho-
tocopying, recording, taping or information storage or re-
trieval systems—without the prior written permission of the
publisher or the author.

Library and Archives Canada Cataloguing in Publication

Omidi, Tom, 1945-
Relationship needs, framework, and models : guidelines
for success / Tom Omidi.

(Love and relationships series ; 5)
ISBN 978-0-9938006-9-6 (paperback)

1. Interpersonal relations. 2. Man-woman relationships.
3. Interpersonal communication. 4. Communication in marriage.
5. Interpersonal conflict. 6. Marital conflict. 7. Conflict management.
8. Couples Psychology. 9. Married people Psychology. I. Title.

HQ801.O455 2016   306.8   C2016-902408-3

Published by Eros Books,
Vancouver, British Columbia
Canada

contact@erosbooks.net

Printed in the United States

Contents

Contents (Cont.)

List of Diagrams and Tables

Introduction

The fast social evolution in recent decades has changed the nature and format of relationships in the new era quite carelessly, to the point where now society itself is threatened by the poor health of relationships. For one thing, the rising level of relationship conflicts is largely responsible for the growing stress level in society, which in turn affects the economy too. The question is how societies can survive if relationships continue to distress the population and cause so much havoc.

Nobody deserves the agonies of marriage breakdown and loneliness. Yet, our own ignorance about relationships' unique needs should be blamed for all the present conundrums. Ultimately, we are responsible for our sufferings in relationships due to our flimsy mentality and approach toward this critical issue. Nevertheless, the rising confusion about relationships is a serious matter, which makes the task of finding new approaches quite urgent.

At two extremes, 'companionship' might feel like a spiritual connection or a boring obligation between partners. We may perceive relationships as a sacred experience in beauty and selflessness, or only a means of social adaptation and self-gratification. While the latter position appears closer to reality, the former reflects our instinctual search for perfection and spirituality. In new societies, people's perceptions of relationships cover both of these extremes and everything else between them. In particular, more people strive nowadays to find their soul mates, while at the same time they are unable to cope even with the basic needs of their relationships. While partners' inner conflicts heighten, they have no clear picture of what relationships are supposed to be (or can actually be).

In all, we have not captured the right sense about the purpose of relationships and how it can be achieved. The reason is that social changes have been too drastic and misleading in recent decades. They have tainted our personalities, perceptions of the world, and expectations from life. We have become too spoiled, needy, and impatient. Meanwhile, our relentless search for a reliable companion, usually with negative experiences and outcomes, causes more stress and confusion.

Unfortunately, we seem helpless to create a balance between practicality and romance. We often fail to use common sense when it is wise to be practical, and we do not know how to express emotions when it can sweeten a relationship. For example, most people have realized that signing a prenuptial agreement is necessary as a practical measure, but doing so still appears businesslike and unromantic. We believe that relationships should begin with romance and trust. Our need for a companion is so strong we commit ourselves prematurely and set high expectations for the success of our relationships too. Ironically, most of us keep thinking all along about the financial consequences of our relationships privately. Especially nowadays, we are too calculating and businesslike about relationships. However, we shyly (or slyly) hide those unromantic thoughts, in order to ease into a relationship that could soothe our mental burdens and insecurities. Deliberately, we ignore the high possibility of separation and all the added pain that relationships usually bring to couples' lives anyway. The truth is that our *urgent* emotional *needs* (e.g., need for sex and attention) overpower our ability to think practically about the potential catastrophes of relationships. This is particularly true because our spirit is usually weakened by other harsh realities of modern lifestyles. We have become too soft and lonely. We also believe that luring in a companion requires a lot of romance, which should not be tainted with matters of practicality. Only afterwards, we become logical (calculating) in running our relationships, while losing sight of all the romance we had felt before. However, all evidences about relationship calamities indicate that we must be doing exactly the opposite, i.e., to be practical first and romantic later.

Obviously, tainted family and social norms are responsible for relationship failures, which in turn damage the society altogether. The only way out of this vicious cycle is to review our vision of relationships and reset it gradually to avoid further social downfall. Our *personal mentality* has to change in order to fit our newer social structure. The *social mentality* about relationships and the government's role must be modified, too, in order to handle the complex nature of new relationships. We need less government interference in relationships, but a more progressive legal system in line with people's modern approach to relationships. Only then, a less hectic relationship environment would reduce the burden on society and the public. The required changes in terms of personal mentality are discussed throughout this book. The required changes in social mentality are also discussed briefly in Chapter Eight. Only with these personal and social changes, we might possibly reverse the fast deteriorating fate of relationships.

Of course, some relationships thrive merely based on partners' mature personalities. Sometimes, one partner may be so enlightened he/she can single-handedly make the relationship flourish. Sometimes, one enlightened partner can bring out the good in his/her partner too. And, of course, sometimes, he/she faces the harshest resistance by his/her partner and actually receives malice despite his/her good intentions. Anyway, the number of relationships flourishing based on partners' goodness is quite small. Thus, the objective in this book is to suggest solutions useful for the large majority of relationships in the new era.

Although many of the suggestions made in this book are partly futuristic in terms of fundamental changes required in both people's mentality and social mechanisms, they provide enough guidelines to improve our relationships right away and benefit from a more tranquil and cooperative relationship environment. We are all capable of changing our mentality gradually and this adjustment would make major impacts on the health of our relationships, while we must also push our governments to consider the fundamental ideas reflected in this book for revamping social mechanisms.

PART I

Relationship
Needs

Chapter One

Relationship Environment

We consider older cultures outmoded mainly in terms of women's demoted status. Obviously, inequality and abuse are intolerable. However, our modern approaches have been unproductive as well. The stress caused by new lifestyles is crippling a good majority of relationships and threatening the foundation of our societies. The situation is only going to get worse if new solutions and a framework for relationships are not found soon.

A major source of relationship conflicts is that couples perceive and define their 'relationship needs' as an extension of their personal needs. Most of us assume that personal needs and relationship needs are the same, or they should coincide. Some people are even more selfish and insist that their personal needs must supersede their partners' needs and any kind of *relationship needs* that might be out there. They try to dominate their partners and set crooked guidelines for their relationships. All along, we all assume that relationships' main (and often 'only') purpose is to make us happy. We expect to find love and a soul mate, which we assume not only are possible to get, but also bring us happiness automatically.

We have no inclination about the nature of relationships in the new era. Instead, we naively trust our perceptions and assumptions, which have gradually grown around our shallow observations and interpretations. We have embraced vast misperceptions about love and happiness all along, which have overwhelmed and paralysed our lives and relationships. Meanwhile, our rising neediness for things and compassion puts extra pressures on relationships. We have developed a huge amount of idiotic needs, in recent decades, over and above our overblown instinctual needs. Meanwhile, society propagates crooked values, including individualism, that push us to become more demanding and arrogant. This trend is growing fast due to people's tendency to imitate others and adopt consumerism too eagerly. Thus, not only we see relationship needs as an extension of our personal needs, but also make many other odd assumptions about the purpose of relationships and our partner's ability and duty to fulfil our expectations.

While struggling with our neediness, misperceptions, and partners' demands, we never give ourselves a chance to do some self-analysis and raise our self-awareness and self-reliance. We get little time, interest, and patience to assess the purposes of our lives and personal habits. Instead, we let our inflated personal needs and whims numb our capacity to envision a practical meaning and purpose for relationships. We ignore that relationships have their own particular needs that if not understood and satisfied, we would never find peace, but only keep fighting with our partners forever.

Obviously, we cannot stop social progress or change people's mentality. Accordingly, the personal needs of individuals will continue to dictate the kind of relationships they are willing to accept for their preferred type of lifestyle. Thus, the meaning, purpose, and format of relationships must be regularly reassessed and redefined along with drastic changes in social trends and values. Yet, so far, we have not had the chance and a mechanism to do so. We have not adapted our relationships to new social values and personal needs of couples. Instead, we simply expect our partners to grasp and satisfy our needs and make us happy, because we have accepted to be in a relationship with them.

Overall, the hectic situation nowadays is due to the lack of a practical framework for our relationships after the fast changes in relationships' environment in recent decades. Parts II and III of this book will study these imbalances and suggest a relationship framework more suitable for the new era. First, however, a deeper understanding about the nature of relationships and our options about this issue is necessary. Ultimately, we have three options:

A. **Continue with the status quo**, hoping that nature will take its course and eventually a format will emerge for relationships. Meanwhile, there will be more separations, conflicts, and paranoia about relationships. The outcome would be rather unpredictable, but surely not satisfactory. The chance that a logical and efficient framework evolves out of this chaos is terribly slim.

B. **Hope that one gender will eventually dominate the other** so that order may return to relationships. Sadly, humans have proven unable to relate to one another and work as a team in the long run, especially the opposite sexes. This is truer nowadays with individualism, arrogance, and greed satiating our mentality and social values. However, the option of one gender taking the superior role in relationships would not work in the end either. Chaos and equality struggles would continue to overwhelm relationships.

C. **Create and propagate a relationship framework** to guide couples run their relationships smoothly and relate efficiently. With the rising social complexity, the longevity of relationships might be doomed anyway. However, a flexible and modern relationship framework could at least do two things: 1) reduce the amount of frictions between couples, and 2) prepare couples for the high likelihood of relationships in the new era failing.

Let us hope the third option would appeal to most of us and we decide to support it actively. Only this option has a chance to bring some level of objectivity back into relationships. In addition, a practical relationship framework could force couples to anticipate, and be mentally prepared for, the reality of separation and living independently. Anyway, this book advocates the third option, as the author believes it would provide the only solution for relationships.

To create a framework for relationships, we must think outside the box and adopt some novel ideas that might initially seem too radical and impractical. However, the readers are encouraged to pause and ponder those ideas, while they wait for more justifications and discussions about the solutions offered in the following chapters. Everything would make total sense if we only try to think realistically and be patient. We must change our mindset about relationships in order to bring relative peace into our lives. We should adopt and support some new ideas, although they contradict our present idealism about relationships. This new mentality would certainly prove essential in the long run for both personal benefits and as part of our social responsibility to reverse the deteriorating state of relationships.

Facts and Trends

Relationship needs must be redefined with time according to the prevailing culture and people's lifestyle choices, as well as their maturity and mentality. Thus, we must study the facts and trends in the new era to grasp the *current* state of relationships. The following dozen trends provide the gist of the matter, but readers could review over 900 facts and trends in the book, *Relationship Facts, Trends, and Choices,* by this author. As a general picture, nevertheless, we can readily observe that:

1. Nowadays, most people do not look for a partner to merely satisfy their basic companionship need. Rather, they want their relationships make them happy and also satisfy a host of their personal needs and/or solve their personal problems. Accordingly, they blame their relationships for their personal failure to figure out life or find happiness.

2. Greed and Ego do not disappear even when couples happen to be in love. In fact, people's growing drive for individualism and equality would boost their greed and Ego. In turn, greed and Ego reinforce all their other pressing needs in relationships, including their needs for identity, control, recognition, love, and retaliation. The point is that love would not eliminate greed and Ego and all the subsequent problems they create in relationships.

3. People are forced to play games and roles all their lives. They are dragged into situations beyond their control to play along with others and assert themselves. This condition infects relationships, too, as partners constantly play games and roles—out of necessity unfortunately. Hardly anybody is natural these days.

4. Couples play games and roles in order to: 1) impress (charm), 2) flatter, 3) intimidate, or 4) snub each other. Therefore, the amount of time they are natural and sincere is too little. Accordingly, the level of mistrust in relationships has increased substantially. Discussions in Chapter Two outlines some of the main reasons for the fast rising mistrust in society and relationships.

5. Personal idiosyncrasies and insecurities have kept rising as social values have deteriorated, and vice versa. This vicious cycle would continue to spin out of control and make the success of relationships less likely every year.

6. The probability of finding our soul mate is extremely slim. However, we all have difficulty accepting this fact, as we want to stay positive. Our romantic search for a soul mate is preventing us from perceiving relationships realistically and facing life as an independent, self-reliant person.

7. For having a suitable companion (let alone a soul mate) partners must have many common interests and compatibility, be good humans, and know how to work on their relationships continuously. However, human nature does not support these requirements. In fact, our modern social values make people more arrogant and needy every day, while the impurity of human nature rises with time, too.

8. Most often, partners actually destroy each other's lives instead of enriching it. This is because life is getting more complex and stressful every year and people have more difficulty coping with social pressures, while they live longer too. The main outcome of this condition is that people are too disturbed and impatient to deal with their excessive relationship demands effectively.

9. We would always face a major trade off in relationships: They always bring us major headaches, whereas for tranquility, we must deal with loneliness and be self-reliant. The dilemma is to make a right decision according to one's personality.

10. All the above facts and hundreds of other reasons explained in this book demonstrate that marriage must be viewed as a temporary arrangement, unless both partners gain all the high qualities required for building an effective relationship.

11. To attain relative tranquility, we must know the art of living independently instead of looking for a soul mate to bring us happiness. For all practical purposes, we must learn to live alone (in the sense of fulfilling our financial and emotional needs personally) instead of looking for relief in relationships.

12. Our only hope is to develop a half dozen or so relationship models that fit couples' varied personalities and needs in line with current culture and couples' mentality. The goal is to provide a relatively tranquil atmosphere for teamwork and effective companionship. This book suggests that only by developing and propagating a relationship framework and its corresponding principles we can achieve this goal. That is the only way to bring some objectivity back into relationships.

The discussions in the following chapters would provide some insight about handling our relationships more thoughtfully in line with the dozen points made above. The objective is to specify relationships' unique needs, which chiefly consist of a set of principles and boundaries to keep partners in a relationship in harmony and minimize frictions between them. The first step for partners would be to understand the perils of their formidable expectations and admit the merits of observing some guidelines in their relationships in line with their needs for more independence and individualism.

Chapter Two

Relationships Reality

A relationship dies, like any entity, if its needs are ignored. Accordingly, we can make the following observations about relationships reality in modern society:

1. Relationships get into trouble because partners are not conscious of its needs and goals or when they find them in major conflict with their personal goals.
2. We should view relationships as an independent entity with specific needs and goals of its own, which are different from partners' personal objectives and needs.
3. Boundaries should be set between partners' personal needs (or goals) and the relationship needs in order to minimize conflicts.
4. A practical framework must be developed to define the needs, objectives, and boundaries of relationships.
5. This relationship framework must also define the characteristics of a successful relationship.
6. As a major role of a relationship framework, it must enforce teamwork and increase the effectiveness of partners' communication.
7. As personal needs change in society, the relationship framework must be adjusted accordingly in order to reduce frictions.

8. Partners' need for independence and individuality should be given the highest priority in developing this relationship framework.

9. The main tool to achieve a balance between personal needs and relationship needs is to reduce couples' expectations from relationships.

10. Like any kind of machinery or system, relationships require routine checks and balances, too, to sustain its functionality.

11. The main challenge for partners is to find the right relationship model for their combined personalities and to function within its parameters. They must stop guessing what a relationship is or what they like it to be.

12. The onus is placed on partners to stay objective and fair by respecting their relationship boundaries in order to prolong their relationship.

Formidable Expectations

Couples' formidable expectations are responsible for the demise of relationship environment in the new era. We have arbitrarily mixed traditional family values with a large amount of new personal ideals and created huge misperceptions in our minds about the purposes and capacity of relationships. This condition cannot prevail if we hope to improve relationships' health. Yet we like our progressive lifestyles and relationships so much nowadays. Thus, the only solution is to at least adjust our mentality about the capacity of relationships, reduce our vast and confusing expectations, and find means of coping with the new reality. Every couple must also choose a proper relationship model suitable for their personalities in terms of the amount of independence and individualism they seek so keenly these days. For achieving even this basis adjustment in our mentality about the reality of relationships in the new era, people must recognize common misperceptions in society that cause ongoing miscommunications and frictions in relationships. In particular, they should grasp the effect of their delusions about trust, commitment, equality, love, happiness, and the role of human hormones.

The Role of Human Hormones

Social chaos in modern societies can be blamed mostly for people's vast misperceptions and attitude regarding happiness, equality, love, trust, and commitment. Furthermore, we can safely blame human hormones for so much of the new relationship conundrums in the new era, while so little ethical and moral principles exist to curb the effects of instinctual and hormonal attributes of humans.

Without getting into too much technical discussions about human hormones, the following scientific facts show the author's overall understanding of hormones' effect on our behaviour and relationships:

- Sexual activity triggers our mood for cuddling and attachment, but the increased sex might erode the sense of attachment in the long run.
- Although attachment might increase sexual urge initially, prolonged attachment often dampens the urge for sex.
- Romance and attachment are not proven to be related.
- Attachment might erode romance.
- Romance might kill sex.
- Humans are not built to be monogamous, unlike some animals that have the right chemistry for it.
- Love often dies within six months to about two years.
- Humans' chemistry (and instincts) draws them to different people for satisfying their romance, sex, attachment urges.
- The effect of human hormones and mood changes, especially for women during childbirth, menstrual cycle, and menopause, contribute largely to gender differences, which contribute to further relationship clashes.

The above facts demonstrate our idealism about humans' ability to honour their marriage commitments, love, monogamy, and to maintain some reasonable amount of trust in their relationships. Many radical conclusions can be drawn in line with these natural human tendencies: On the one hand, the effects of hormones on our behaviour in a sense suggest that we should not really feel too guilty for being so sexually inclined and losing our willpower to honour our wedding vows and relationship commitments. They also suggest that we should not get too mad and frustrated with our cheating spouses, either, if we could logically see their helplessness about all these tricks of Nature. On the other hand, we cannot stop wondering about humans' ability to be a bit more ethical and have some level of self-control, despite all their natural tendencies. What kind of society and relationship atmosphere we humans really need and can support?

Trust

The level of mistrust in society and relationships is rising too fast due to our devious hormones, our bad experiences, and social environment in the new era. Obviously, the success of a relationship depends on the goodness of its partners. However, individuals' characteristics, actions, and nature reveal the inherent shortfalls of humans, especially for socializing. In fact, it might be easier to prove that humans become more arrogant and unreliable the more they socialize and as time goes by. Thus, it becomes harder for them to relate and get along in relationships and communities. All the facts show that the chances of creating even a small society of pure humans are slim, because they would not be left alone to choose their way of life. Developing a pure man within the crooked value systems of modern society simply appears like a funny concept. It sounds like a plan to nurture edible fish in a contaminated swamp. With the speed we are destroying the environment, where nature is supposed to flourish itself and embrace us too, how could a puritan emerge?

These conclusions are again depressing in terms of human relationships. They only confirm humans' limitations to understand the requirements of relationships and coping with them. On the other hand, if we accept that human nature is impure, we also learn to keep our expectations from people and relationships low. We get less surprised and angry while we develop some form of understanding and compassion toward our partners and helpless humanity.

Obviously, it may benefit us psychologically to assume that we can try to become better human beings than we have so far been. We know that we have spiritual tendencies. We know that with meditation we can find some level of awareness and thus tranquility. However, are we made to be a peaceful and logical species? Do we really understand 'logic'? Does our logic and common sense have any meaning or significance? It is hard to judge. But I doubt it personally. We have not yet been able to demonstrate such capacity. Yet, since human is not inherently pure, perhaps we should strive even harder, against our nature, to become a bit purer in order to serve ourselves in such a harsh social environment.

Nevertheless, we must adjust our mentality about mistrust in relationships in a productive manner by considering the following points:

1. Our accurate perceptions of corruption and duplicity in society cause cynicism about people's truthfulness and authenticity. This personal wisdom and warranted defence mechanism might inadvertently lead to a large level of misperceptions in relationships. Many misperceptions are also caused by our idiosyncrasies or communication hurdles.

2. The high percentage and repercussions of marriage breakdowns simply make relationships too risky in the new era. Thus, absolute caution regarding the words and promises of our partners seems quite warranted.

3. Mistrust is a natural (and often necessary) condition in relationships in the new era. This is a logical consequence of social life and not a sign of a person's weakness or selfishness. However, partners' mistrust is often caused by their own oversensitivity and misperceptions, too, which then affects their behaviour and their partner's added mistrust in them. In all, partners must remain conscious of the high possibility, and many causes, of misjudging each other.
4. We must stop expecting our partners to trust us completely, especially when we honestly feel the difficulty of doing the same thing ourselves.
5. We can never know *who we are* or *who they are* and they can never know *who they are* or *who we are*. We must honour these two facts with an open mind. We struggle all our lives to find ourselves and happiness, to no avail. So how can we expect others to know us and trust us when even we do not? It is simply impossible to build complete trust based on our doubtful perceptions of ourselves and others.
6. We should not consider love and trust as the main factors of relationships' health anymore. This is a deceptive, illogical yardstick. People often lie about their love or trust to avoid confrontations, or merely for being tactful and wise. Expecting trust or love beyond people's natural capacity would only bring more duplicity and phoniness into relationships.
7. We must come to terms with two major facts in the new era: 1) it is natural that couples lose trust in each other to some extent eventually, and 2) we should learn to live in relationships with imperfect trust levels instead of making a big issue out of it. We should be ultra cautious at the time of starting our relationships, but then remain flexible about inevitable mistrust and disappointments later on.

The fact that we must try so hard to become better human beings and find happiness shows that humans are not pure by nature and they are not trustworthy. On the other hand, acknowledging our impurity should motivate us to overcome our Egos and try harder to understand the meaning and process of becoming a better human; not merely because it would be a social ideal, but because it would make us happier at the end. The simple fact that the Ego is an inherent part of the human psyche is enough to cause human bias, selfishness, hypocrisy, and hundreds of other flaws. The fact that we are so greedy and competitive, and the way we love capitalism, materialism, and pleasures show that we are impure by nature. The fact that Christians believe Jesus died because of their sins—and similar beliefs in other religions—shows humans' tendency to sin. The fact that so many relationships fail nowadays, and the way partners treat each other at the time of separation, show their impurity; it also shows people's inability to get along, trust one another, and show compassion. The fact that we must constantly go for confessions and repentance, to cleanse our souls, is another clue about our impurity. The fact that we do good things and charity (often for self-serving purposes, to cleanse our conscience, or for pretension) does not wash all other negative tendencies that exist in human nature. Purity is not a matter of comparing the number of good deeds versus bad ones either, even if people did more good than bad. Purity is an absolute fact and not an algebraic equation. It either exists or not. Even doing one bad thing indicates the impurity of human nature. We must be blind not to see it at such a high dosage. The only question is how often humans' impurity reaches evilness. Too often and globally, it usually feels! As we feel all these impurities around us, keeping our trust in others, even our family members, has become a very tough job.

Commitment

Along with the above discussions about mistrust in relationships and human nature in general, it is clear that relying on our partners, or even their promises, would be rather naïve.

Accordingly, expecting them to fulfil their commitments, especially in terms of staying in their relationships, does not sound like a wise strategy for anybody. Yet, deep down, we all imagine that relationships' longevity is still a valid expectation in the new era. Due to our traditional mentality, one major misperception in society and people's minds is that relationships should last forever. Nowadays, however, this is the least likely scenario considering the statistics on divorce, family problems, strive for individualism, sexuality, and the increasing level of stress in society. So now, it is time to perceive relationships more in terms of an open-ended arrangement rather than a long-term commitment. In the author's opinion, we should indeed look forward with great excitement to propagating this rather radical mindset. The reason is that the advantages of such a relationship arrangement might amaze us in the end. This would prove to be one of those unique instances where reverse psychology would prove to work extremely well. The couples' knowledge that their relationship would terminate *automatically*, at a certain point, would make them stay together much longer than would be possible under the present circumstance. They simply stay vigilant and protect their relationship in a constructive, teamwork environment. They realize that they must work on their relationship regularly to maintain it instead of taking it for granted and letting it expire at a preset date. This reverse psychology would definitely help our societies in at least four ways:

- Couples get into their relationships more carefully based on intelligent analyses of their needs, compatibility, and the suitability of a particular relationship model for them.
- Couples work harder and more consciously to prolong their relationships instead of letting it expire. This would most likely increase the longevity of most relationships that are worth saving.
- Couples are mentally prepared to leave their relationships with the least amount of shock and hassle when a relation-

ship is not working. They know from the beginning that, if necessary, separation is a good and acceptable possibility.
• Ending relationships is automatic and hassle free.

The point is that we need modern thinking and principles for relationships to match the modern life we are so eagerly embracing. Along with our new lifestyles and thirst for individualism, we would also behave more in line with the humans' innate sexual tendencies and hormones noted above. We are addressing our sexuality more liberally every day with lesser concern about social ethics, anyway. Thus, viewing relationships as a temporary arrangement may be the only logical solution for the dilemma of relationships, considering the rising rate of relationship failures, our sizzling sexuality, and our eagerness to have a companion, too, anyway. If we learn to perceive relationships *only* as a conditional companionship, which might entail a family too, then we can possibly define a set of relationship principles more appropriate for the modern life and then set our expectations accordingly.

Some people have already reached similar conclusions and are building their relationships more freely. They are not concerned about marriage formalities, such as a license or a church wedding. In another type of relationships, mostly prevalent in developing societies (where romantic imaginations have not corrupted partners' cultural view of relationships), couples still depend on tradition or religious principles to maintain their relationships. However, the rest of us believe that neither of these kinds of relationships is appropriate. We disapprove these approaches since partners are not bound by official documents or they are not marrying based on love. We perceive these relationships valueless, because in our modern thinking we have learned to focus on relationships as a love-union. Yet, at the same time, we insist on legal documents and court system to protect us when love erodes. We all know that our naive love has a good chance of faltering sooner or later.

Yet, we insist on ignoring this information at the outset. It is a big irony that we wish to base our marriages on love and trust, but in fact do not trust each other's promise to live together merely on the strength of the presumed love. We want a marriage license and legal protection. Love without trust! This is hypocritical but also an obvious contradiction. It shows our hunch about the high risks of both love and relationships nowadays. We insist on legal protection for the possibility of the marriage breakdown, but we are too shy and romantic to sign a contract that dictates partners' rights upon their marriage breakdown without any need to go to court.

Equality

Nowadays, we try to oversimplify, perhaps even abuse, the interworking of relationships by pushing the concept of equality and assuming that all the problems would be solved automatically. We attempted to solve women's personal problems and reduce the amount of intimidation and control by men. However, we have not solved the problems of relationships. In fact, it appears that relationship conflicts have increased dramatically in society the more this concept of equality has been emphasized and enforced. Even worse, women's frustration has increased due to their unfulfilled expectations. The more they have expected from their relationships, the less they have actually ended up receiving (again judging by divorce rates and increasing family conflicts).

Often, women's expectations for equality appear vague, sounding more like whining, with devastating effect on their relationships. Some women's exaggerated demand for equality sometimes looks more like a quest for superiority. Initially, the equality movement sounded logical for overcoming men's superiority. But now, everything appears to be turning around. That is, men feel unequal in a world where women set most standards of equality, which appear one-sided or arbitrary.

They often feel intimidated by their partners' ambiguous expectations. Many of them have adopted a passive role in their relationships due to the severity of their spouses' views of equality. The problem is that, nowadays, 'equality bargaining' is infected by partners' Ego.

Equality expectations often arise from partners' urge to control one another. The concept of equality is psychologically absurd anyway. This is because everyone inherently believes that his/her logic is superior to other people's, including his/her criteria for defining equality. We strongly believe that we know about everything better than everybody else regardless of their genders. A strong tendency exists in most humans to feel superior to others, not equal, although they might pretend to be fair and humble. In modern societies, almost everybody believes in gender equality, but not intellectual equality. By default, our Ego forces us to feel almost perfect in terms of logic, intelligence, cognition and all the rest of the good stuff. The gender equality issue is resolved for the most part, but the inherent sense of superiority can never be erased from people's minds—due to their innate perception of their intellectual superiority. This is the source of all the inequalities nowadays. They are not gender driven but rather Ego driven for both genders. Gender equality is a hot issue nowadays due to the relationships' rising importance and troubles in society, and because everybody (men and women) feels special and superior and not equal.

Equality is, by the way, perceived and measured differently by people according to their subjective criteria and emotional maturity. Thus, instead of wasting so much energy on forcing some kind of imaginary equality in relationships, couples must learn to put all those efforts into defining a practical process of teamwork. Teamwork enables couples to contribute to major decisions and feel active in their relationships. However, it does not deprive partners from doing most tasks independently based on their expertise or merely for creating synergy. Partners should be able to decide independently, instead of doubting their authority or identity all the time according to some fake rules of equality. They should not lose their confidence and the control of their lives in fear of retaliation.

The concept of 'equality' has initially emerged out of a sense of desperation, but is now being driven mostly by Ego—the urge for superiority. Teamwork, on the other hand, is Self (goodness) and Model (tactfulness) driven. Therefore, it is not too difficult to decide which approach could have a better chance of success in the long run. Couples' quarrels to exert equality would only reinforce the Egos of both partners, which would only lead to more clashes. Besides, as said before, the concept of equality is psychologically flawed anyway, because our prominent Ego absolutely abhors equality. People are psychologically incapable of handling equality because they feel superior in their deepest level of consciousness.

Love

In the recent decades, couples have suddenly become too romantic, but also too antagonistic. Everyone believes that love should be the foundation of relationships. In this sense, life has become a big theatre. Everybody tries to be romantic. And they expect their partners to be equally good in romance, too, as a test of their commitment. But then they retaliate harshly, and show their evil side, when love fades away—which happens regularly in most relationships. They turn separation into such a calamity when they realize that their supposedly initial love had been a farce. They make life hell for themselves and their partners because love has evaporated (if there had been any real love to begin with). Now couples turn into ferocious adversaries accusing each other of lying about their earlier love promises. They curse their partners for not loving them anymore, as if love were something to force upon oneself and not a natural phenomenon. They find their partners responsible for the lost love, even if they are the ones feeling out of love. Actually, they often blame their partners for making them fall out of love. They accuse their partners of having killed their love. They also blame them for their loss of youth. These past lovers now suddenly view each other as criminals deserving a severe punishment, including a difficult and costly separation. The penalty for falling out of love is too horrendous nowadays. Therefore, some people continue to play the role of a romantic fool to keep the situation under control. They accept the humiliation of submitting to their spouses' whims to stop their whining, and because the penalties, financially and emotionally, for ending relationships are too high. Nevertheless, most of us still feel obliged to be romantic, just to keep up with social norms and expectations.

Almost everybody finally admits that love, in the sense they had initially imagined it, is a transitory state. Then they may decide that the option of staying in loveless relationships, against their convictions, is preferable to loneliness or high penalties of separation. However, now they do not know how to handle a relationship that is not defined by love. They believe their relationship has failed and has no value. Some may seek love in another person's arms; to find the love they believe they deserve.

Everybody believes he/she deserves love and must find it somehow. Yet, we all ignore a simple fact about the meaning of love: That the more one seeks selfless love (SLove), the more one must be honest and sincere in character. At the same time, it is becoming more difficult to be honest and sincere nowadays, because of all the games introduced in relationships. Of course, we imagine that we can hide our insincerity, mistrust, and dishonesty from the rest of the world. However, this mentality only shows our arrogance and trust in our pretentious personality (Model) to bail us out. The good news is that people can largely see each other's true nature despite all the elaborate games they play to portray a false personality of themselves and to conceal their calculating nature. In all, the games and retaliation schemes in relationships show how ridiculous the idea of measuring the strength of our relationships by love is. We just ignore all these contradictions and keep looking for SLove in such a contaminated environment.

Nevertheless, many of us face a big dilemma: On the one hand, getting out of relationships proves excruciating, in terms of the hardships imposed by our partners and society (the judicial system in particular). On the other hand, many couples are frustrated and confused, nowadays, because they feel trapped in their loveless (usually hostile) relationships. The situation is in particular stressful for persons who really believe that love is the essence of relationships. Even worse, many couples have to continue playing some phony roles that marriage counsellors tell them to play in order to save their relationships.

Our present mindset reflects our lack of clarity about the nature of love and its role in relationships. Overall, we insist that relationships, and its survival, must be justified and driven by love. In the contemporary definition of relationships, our culture permeates many invalid myths. We believe that:

- Love is the test of relationships' success.
- Love lasts forever.
- Love makes a relationship last forever.
- Relationships must be validated by love.
- Relationships thrive on love.
- Anybody considering a serious relationship should and would find a person to exchange love with each other.
- Expressing love regularly guarantees relationships' success.
- Love is a common phenomenon that everyone understands and is capable of delivering.
- Love is a common commodity that everyone must find and enjoy in his/her life.

- When there is love, relationship problems are rare and manageable.
- Love overcomes all the relationship problems.
- Partners can control over their feelings to love each other forever.

These myths are furthest from the nature of relationships in the new era. Love does not have the meaning or the power stipulated in the above myths. Nor do relationships necessarily last longer if partners start their relationships with love. We are not learning any lesson from the fact that most relationships in the modern world have started based on *some kind of love* and they still keep failing miserably. It is amazing.

The scientific evidence about the role of human hormones on our behaviour is another proof of our misperception about the power of love. Maybe it is all right to seek love so eagerly. However, we should also remember the flimsy nature of love in general, as well as the chaotic nature of relationships in the new era. We should do so to be prepared for the consequences of our futile search for love or even finding it. We should indeed concentrate on developing our 'self' (selflessness) instead of indulging ourselves with more love deficiency and phony lovers. Besides, pure love happens by accident and not active search.

Another cause for misperception in relationships is that partners use love as another yardstick for measuring equality. That is, they expect their partners to love them as much as they think (or pretend) they love their partners. They demand love-equality to ensure the fairness of their relationships. Obviously, love-equality is a symptom of the general equality craze in society. People believe that love is a spiritual feeling, but then make it totally conditional on their partners' ability to love them equally. With their demands for love and equality, they simply expose their selfishness (instead of selflessness) and destroy their chances to relax and relate naturally.

Couples' perceptions and expressions of love are clearly not selfless as long as they insist on love equality. It is even more bizarre when they often retaliate harshly when they do not perceive the love they get adequate. How can this attitude have any trace of spiritual love in it? It is at best only a phoney love (where partners try to play the role of lovers), without any sense of selflessness (needlessness for equality). This is clearly an example of partners' increasing confusion every day about their perceptions of love, which then leads to more expectations from relationships. The need for equality has become such an imposing social phenomenon that it has even infected our love affairs. We are less interested in figuring out how our partners' integrity may qualify them as our soul mates. Nobody knows what the characteristics of a soul mate should be. Rather, we insist on measuring, in greatest accuracy, the equality (as well as the intensity) of the love our partners can show, which we continue to doubt anyway.

While equality, in the sense of *fairness,* is the foundation of our democratic society, it has turned into a socio-political platform to further spread our demented social values. The term 'equality' is somewhat misused inadvertently to express our repressed anxieties, which then leads to creation of new expectations and headaches. Unfortunately, the meaning and implication of equality are often exaggerated, so much so it has ruined the structure of relationships altogether.

Obviously, relationships' chances of survival have declined drastically with love becoming the main success factor—because love itself cannot survive in relationships. In fact, a cynical interpretation of *love* implies that it flourishes only by deprivation and not through a relationship. Perhaps believing that relationships (marriage) kill(s) love is cynical. However, we can safely say that after the initial stages of companionship, couples encounter a special atmosphere dissimilar to their initial perceptions of *love*. The new atmosphere is shaped according to the peculiar personal needs and personalities of partners, which is hardly ever spiritual or logical. Therefore, in light of all these clues, both a more meaningful view of love and a better perspective of relationships is useful for resolving some of our misperceptions. The question is why should not our culture focus on factors that are effective in prolonging relationships without depending on love too much? And the question is why we cannot identify these relevant factors of success for relationships? The answer is that we really do not appreciate the true nature of love and relationships in the present era. And we have not yet realized the importance of developing a relationship framework.

Many of us might realize eventually that our perceptions of an ideal relationship are unrealistic and then lower our expectations. We may end up thinking *practical* at the end, but not before hurting ourselves and our partners for a long time with our misperceptions. Often it would be too late anyway. Nowadays, the term 'practical' feels mostly like a type of submission, 'a sense of resignation and disappointment,' that eventually prevails in relationships nowadays. Most relationships contain good doses of resignation and disappointment. However, we could have a 'practical' and productive relationship if we set our mindsets right. Instead, many people may lose good companionship opportunities due to their unrealistic demands. They destroy their marriages or look for an idol until most of their useful lives are wasted on dreams. Some of them might then further damage their pride, integrity, and convictions when they keep downgrading their expectations drastically for the sake of getting into a relationship quickly despite its obvious flaws and predictable headaches.

Happiness

Happiness is a myth all by itself, but finding it in relationships is plain utopian. We have difficulty even defining happiness because it is not a stable state or experience. We only perceive it as an everlasting state of joy and tranquility, which we also expect to result from our endless materialistic desires, greed, and competition. This is a fundamental contradiction already. We want happiness to fit our contaminated lifestyles, instead of a lifestyle that could induce peace of mind as the closest state of happiness. We forget that any chance for happiness requires a drastic change of personal lifestyle (mainly toward selflessness), which only a few of us might eventually find the courage to effect.

Besides, human nature does not support happiness and tranquility because of innate human urges for challenge, controversy, power, domination, competition, greed, struggle for survival, etc. Anger, hatred, jealousy, spite, and aggression come to us so naturally, but we must try really hard to be honest, compassionate, sincere, and all the other good stuff. Life is not a happy journey either. Our occasional taste of happiness and tranquility soon faces new dilemmas and disappointments. Thus, as a main step for finding some tranquility and improving our relationships, we must actually learn that happiness is a myth and not a stable state.

In relationships, the notion of happiness becomes particularly too idealistic, because partners expect each other and their relationship to satisfy their illusory perceptions of happiness, including their egotistical and materialistic needs, pleasure, sexuality, and everlasting tranquility. This expectation is actually one major cause of relationship breakdowns. Partners deprive themselves from the basic privileges of relationships because they believe relationships are meant to bring them happiness. They cause themselves more suffering with their obsession for happiness. This is an ironic condition we have brought upon ourselves in recent decades. Instead of learning selflessness and contentment, partners try to strengthen their identities in relationships through arrogance, and then expect happiness too.

Furthermore, most of us mistake pleasures (especially sexuality) with happiness, or assume that more pleasures lead to happiness. So, most relationships become instable soon enough, only because they fail to satisfy our fantastic appetite for happiness and sexuality. Of course, we cannot avoid the impression that companionship can fulfil a large number of our personal needs. However, depending on others or relationships to satisfy our personal needs and bring us happiness is naïve and the leading cause of our suffering. For getting even a chance to taste this elusive happiness, we must seek it within ourselves according to our mental capacity and awareness.

Happiness is a complex topic for discussion, especially within the context of our crooked social values. Many books are written on this topic and maybe another one is due to explain the connection between happiness and relationships in more details than are possible in this book. A great collection of happiness definitions can be found in *Happiness*, Perennial Books, 2014. This author's book, *the Mysteries of Life, Love, and Happiness*, is also a good source for learning about this topic.

The natural conclusion in most 'happiness' books is that it may be found only inside a person and he/she needs a special mindset to understand and effect this state. This is what this book advocates as well with an emphasis on becoming better humans through personal awareness, to contact our spirit and become needless about many artificial facets of life in the new era. However, this book also emphasizes on staying practical and understanding our humanistic limitations, which hinder our efforts to be content and a better person.

Some books (quoting philosophers, Buddhism, and the Dalai Lama) suggest that the purpose of life is to find happiness. This is a notion that this author has some reservations about, because he believes that life does not have a purpose by itself and humans have many other ambitions besides happiness. The purpose of life (in the context of creation) is neither to spread happiness nor to create good human beings. Happiness is not even the purpose of one's life (regardless of the purpose of the universe). Life is merely a collection of events and moments that transpires in people's lives according to natural laws and chances and affects them based on their cognition (i.e., beliefs, awareness, intelligence, etc.). We all prefer happiness because suffering hurts, and not because it is the purpose of life. We have many higher ambitions in life that we often pursue with greater passion than our desire for happiness or even pleasures, e.g., need for love, power, or recognition. Most of us just cannot sit idle and be happy with our contentment. We resent boredom and we want more adventures even if they cause suffering. We want to be loved even though it often leads to disappointment and pain. The point is that we are not born to be happy or good humans and these are not the purposes of life. We want to become better human beings to soothe our hurts, release tension, or because we sometimes prefer (or like to pretend) to be at peace with ourselves and our surroundings. Happiness and goodness are the probable outcomes of our personal choices to set the right balance between our ambitions and contentment. Life does not have any particular meaning, nor is it about anything in particular. Even if life is about something or has a meaning, God has not yet revealed it to us through His prophets, nor has He given us enough intelligence to figure it out.

The slogan 'life is for the purpose of happiness' is in fact causing more suffering than guiding people toward happiness. The reason is that it makes people believe that such a myth (happiness) actually exists, and that the reason they cannot find it is due to their stupidity or relationships. They feel incompetent and frustrated. They leave their relationships prematurely or seek all kinds of pleasures and sexuality to attain the purpose of life, i.e., happiness. But then they feel even more empty and lost.

Most importantly, life is not for the purpose of getting hung up over a mythical concept like happiness and causing extra suffering for ourselves. Ninety-nine percent of us cannot find that elusive happiness. The one percent who claims to have found it, like monks and priests, must make many sacrifices, limit their social activities, and accept celibacy and suffering in order to maintain their state of contentment, which they call happiness. It seems that happiness has a lot to do with selflessness, meditation, celibacy, and absorbing sufferings. However, by nature, most of us are selfish, and like our sexuality and pleasures a lot, which would accordingly lead to unhappiness. How many of us are willing to be celibate, limit our pleasures and social lives, and welcome sufferings to reach the height of enlightenment (for happiness)? We have to really force ourselves to fulfil most of these requirements, which shows happiness can never be a natural pursuit of humans, especially in our materialistic world. Accordingly, the purpose of our existence is not to seek happiness, as the Dalai Lama says, because we humans are not prepared to pay the price for it and we are not made for it. We must think and act within our natural capacities, while aiming to be better human beings too. In particular, blaming our relationships and partners for not stirring the happiness that we cannot find anywhere else on our own is a silly attitude prevalent in society nowadays.

Ironically, the fact that we crave happiness in vain reveals our inner turmoil and inability to define our existence in simpler terms personally.

Chapter Three

Successful Relationships

A successful relationship develops automatically when both partners are *good* and *enlightened*. 'Good' refers to partners' ability to be natural, rely more on their conscience and Self, and less on Ego, for relating to each other. 'Enlightened' means that partners are aware of humans' inherent limitations and have low expectations from relationships. They realize their own flaws and sympathize with their partners for being crippled by the same inner and outer forces beyond their control.

These tough conditions drastically restrict the opportunity for building good relationships nowadays, considering the difficulty of being good and enlightened individuals. The possibility of both partners being good and enlightened is even more remote. Just the opposite: Our genetic defects, sexuality, and the negative impacts of social and family environments, make us rigid with huge Egos. We are crippled by our grave misperceptions about life values and who we are. Therefore, we seldom give ourselves a chance to learn about some of the finer means of thinking and living. Even when we do, we have extreme difficulty staying on a path of awareness when people around us are consumed with superficial needs and spread phony values. For example, it is too difficult to resist the niceties of 'consumerism' when the whole world is embracing it so dearly. It is hard to overcome one's obsession for 'equality' and show enough patience for teamwork. How could one not adopt these progressive and seemingly rational ideologies? How could one explain one's passivity and modesty to one's obsessed companion or friends? One's Ego and need for compliance would not allow it. These examples are not meant to undermine the need for 'equality' or to criticize consumerism. Rather, they reflect that social trends usually override even our purest personal beliefs, logic, or good intentions. Thus, we must find relationship solutions that fit the emerging, irreversible course of history.

We must now view relationships in a new light. We need new approaches to empower relationships. The new objectives must correspond with our new social structure and our increasing demand for independence and individuality. Instead of looking for an ideal, imaginary relationship environment, our new goal should be to make relationships only manageable and tolerable. It is time to lower our expectations and define new objectives for our relationships. Finding a workable framework is an ambitious goal, but if we are lucky and lucid we may be able to create a balance between our personal needs and relationship needs.

No one really knows the parameters of a successful relationship due to rapid social changes that have tainted most people's perceptions, personalities, and their relationships. Therefore, we usually list out some relationship objectives, such as love, security, longevity, and wealth, as indicators of its success. We also consider 'communication' an important factor for the success of relationships. Those who have had bad experiences in relationships are quite cynical about the possibility of building successful relationships. To them, relationships can be nothing but hell.

In the absence of a guideline, we create our own subjective perceptions about the purposes and potentials of relationships based on our personal needs and superficial values around us. We create a fantasy in our heads about the nature of relationships and their success indicators. Accordingly, we set ourselves up for disappointment, because our naïve expectations cannot be fulfilled. Chapter Two shows some of our main misperceptions about relationships. The bottom line is that we (as a society) no longer have a common understanding of relationships and its purposes, let alone a grasp of the factors making them successful. Our educational systems, especially at senior high school, have failed to teach this vital real life subject to the group of people who need this knowledge so urgently. It is a pity that such an important matter, with such grave effect on social wellbeing, is left to personal interpretations instead of being researched for everybody's benefit.

Therefore, to study relationships, we must develop, 1) a definition of it, 2) a list of success factors for it, and 3) a realistic list of partners' expectations from it.

A Definition of Relationships

We can say that, a relationship is mainly a collection of activities and feelings shared by partners. However, a relationship must also be viewed as a system or atmosphere for facilitating partners' cooperation to achieve certain goals. These goals are of two kinds: First, the goals that fulfil the realistic personal and common needs of partners. Second, the goals that help maintain the health of the relationship itself.

Thus, a comprehensive definition is:

A *relationship is a system or atmosphere with specific needs and goals to sustain itself, which only then might fulfil partners' realistic goals too.*

This definition places the emphasis on relationship needs and goals before a relationship can be of any use to couples. Obviously, to deal with the existing chaos, couples must show willingness and patience to learn about the relationships' special needs. They must view 'relationships' as a unique entity with specific needs. Surely, the process of acknowledging and applying this principle to relationships would be gradual, because couples must learn to reduce their expectations from relationships and attend to their personal needs more independently. Thus, the first thing we must study is the viability of people's expectations from relationships in the new era.

A Review of Relationship Expectations

To develop a realistic list of relationship expectations for the new era, we can start with a list of couples' ideal, common expectations, as shown in Table 3.1. Then we can discuss and eliminate the ones that are too conflicting with partners' personal needs. After all, relationships nowadays should accommodate couples' craving for independence and individuality.

**Table 3.1: A Preliminary List of
General Expectations from Relationships**

1. Sex
2. Dependence- support
3. Financial Security
4. Communication
5. Compassion
6. Companionship
7. Teamwork
8. Love: SLove, ELove, MLove
9. Trust
10. Happiness – Peace of mind, tranquility, joy
11. Friendship – Loyalty, honesty, etc.
12. Respect- Social acceptance
13. Personal Success
14. Commitment
15. Longevity

An ideal relationship would satisfy all the expectations in Table 3.1 and more. However, we must aim only for the ones that can fit the majority of relationships according to our present mentalities and lifestyles. Discussions in the following pages will show why many of these expectations are hard to achieve nowadays; and thus the need to exclude them in order to reduce the useless pressures on relationships and to minimize partners' disappointments. This would be contrary to what couples are in fact doing nowadays, as they assume relationship expectations can be a natural extension of their rising personal needs. As society promotes phonier lifestyles, the level and complexity of partners' expectations have kept rising. Everybody believes s/he deserves to live like movie stars. However, the reality is just the opposite. That is, the level of expectations from relationships must be reduced to compensate for the growing pressures that society is placing on the personal lives of people already. They have enough headaches outside the house without the need for more pressures from their relationships too. But they should also reduce their expectations in line with their rising emphasis on personal identity, independence, and individualism. In some special cases, all the expectations in Table 3.1 may be fulfilled in a relationship. However, as a rule, we must satisfy most of these personal needs independently. Now let us review the expectations listed in Table 3.1 and pinpoint the unrealistic ones.

1. Sex: This is the most reasonable expectation from relationships. Since couples *attempt* not to look outside their relationships to fulfil this urge, they must depend on their relationships to satisfy this essential need. In reality, however, partners often withdraw sex as a tool for emotional blackmail or retaliation. In addition, sometimes partners cannot cooperate in this regard and thus look for sex elsewhere. Nonetheless, nothing can be done about this need beyond what everybody already knows and practices the best way they can. This is a legitimate expectation from relationships. All other dramas surrounding sex cannot be helped either. Most of them are psychologically explainable and rather inevitable. The only advice is to learn about the role of sex more realistically instead of using it for blackmailing and hurting our partners.

2. Dependence: Partners' attempt to create a balance between their needs for both dependence and independence create a great deal of inner conflicts for them while complicating their relationship too. We get into relationships in most cases for relieving our loneliness. We need to depend on a partner to make our lives easier. However, in reality, many relationships make partners feel the ultimate sense of loneliness. Maybe the sense of physical loneliness is remedied somewhat by living under the same roof with a partner. However, psychological loneliness reaches its height when partners fail to relate and communicate. Relationships enhance our sense of loneliness many folds, because we feel the difficulty of relating to another person tangibly, and because we had imagined we could do all that rather easily, mostly on the power of love alone. Most of us had never felt so desperate and lonely psychologically when we were living alone. We are terribly disappointed after all the years of daydreaming about finding a partner to relieve our loneliness. Therefore, depending on our partners to cure our psychological loneliness is an unreasonable expectation.

Another hurdle is that even if our partners were capable of satisfying our need for dependence, we personally sabotage their willingness by our constant expressions of individualism and independence. Our false pride prevents us from expressing our need for dependence and our partner's moral support directly. Instead, we pretend quite strongly to be emotionally self-reliant. Showing our neediness could tilt the balance of power in relationship after all. Meanwhile, we strive to fulfil both our dependence and independence needs just by playing some superficial roles and expecting our partners to understand their meanings and also respond favourably. However, these conflicting (unexpressed) expectations and role-playing only frustrate our partners. They recall our previous shows of independence, especially when we suddenly play the role of a vulnerable partner seeking dependence. Showing the right balance of dependence and independence and clarifying the timing and areas where we need our partners' support is difficult. We might imagine that we are doing a good job of it, but that is only another selfish assumption and gross misperception.

Our struggle for independence and dependence makes us jittery regularly. Thus, we react unfavourably toward our partners, unjustifiably, especially when we assume they are refusing to understand our needs intentionally. Naturally, when a partner seeks independence and finds his/her partner a hurdle in achieving it, he/she feels frustrated and resentful toward his/her partner. And he/she gets frustrated, too, when he/she needs attention and dependence and the partner is not available or capable of providing it. The situation gets out of hand as relationships remain undefined in terms of dependency and independency needs of partners.

Of course, showing compassion always helps the health (and dependency needs) of relationships when couples notice their partners' need for dependence despite their arrogant show of independence. It is a good gesture by partners to stay civilized toward each other in those circumstances. However, when we keep switching between our independence and dependence urges and roles in relationships, we should also expect that our partners lose their sensitivity and true sympathy about our needs. Meanwhile, partners' personal tension heightens while they are unaware of the ongoing competition between their conflicting needs for independence and dependence. They sense only their partners' indifference toward their needs even when they continue to play a variety of idiotic roles themselves, including retaliation, to draw their attention.

Overall, each partner has difficulty understanding and responding to his/her partner's incongruent expectations for dependence and independence. He/she is also frustrated when his/her own needs for dependence and independence are not satisfied. These dual deprivations lead to many personal (inner) conflicts for him/her already. However, partners' inner conflicts heighten when their needs for dependence and independence do not coincide in terms of timing and partners' mood fluctuations. It hurts them deeply, since their natural (instinctual) personal needs for dependence and independence are badly imbalanced and ignored. This gross incongruity causes constant frictions between partners while they criticize each other's erratic needs, too. All along, partners' rotating struggles for more freedom or more attention come across as unnatural and sinister. The situation makes both partners believe that his/her partner is instable or neurotic. They also feel that their partners are placing these expectations on their relationship illogically or even out of spite. Therefore, instead of understanding and *dealing with it logically*, they react negatively by retaliation and confrontation.

Nonetheless, it is difficult to deal with the unrealistic expectations of our partners for dependence and independence; especially in the eyes of an impatient partner who is unwilling or unable to cope with such conflicting needs (and demands) so frequently. The irony is that people's needs for both dependence and independence are increasing simultaneously every day. As noted before, people are getting too spoiled and needy due to the effect of complex social values. They ask for more compassion (dependence) while also demand more freedom and identity (independence). Of course, when partners accuse each other of behaving erratically, they face only more arguments and frustrations. Thus, instead of discussing their relationship dilemmas calmly and objectively, they focus only on dominating the situation and each other, or opt for separation. They see no option other than either adapting to this confusing environment or getting out of the relationship altogether. Both options are obviously destructive.

In our modern way of thinking, we accept open-mindedly that both dependence and independence are essential needs, and we naively believe we can cope with this major dilemma in our relationships. We might even assume that by some magical power we would find the right balance (between our needs for dependence and independence). We assume we can make compromises so that both partners can fulfil their rotating needs for independence and dependence by common sense. This is a highly unrealistic expectation.

Partners' erratic attempts to be dependent or independent confuse them, especially when they do not get the responses they expect. Accordingly, relationship mechanisms, including communication, stop working. So what is the solution? Since our emphasis nowadays is placed on individualism and independence, we must adjust our expectations from relationships accordingly. That is, **we should stick to independence and assume that relationships are no longer capable of satisfying our need for dependence at the desired level.** We must also prepare ourselves to deal with our inner conflicts (caused by inadequate dependence) without blaming our partners. Many readers might object: 'What is the point of being in a relationship if partners cannot depend on each other totally?' This is a valid question that is answered in the future chapters. However, the bottom line is that we cannot really demand independence so strongly and also seek dependence. This does not make sense. Analysing this complex puzzle is what this book is all about. We may still count on our partners' integrity, cooperation, support, and teamwork, but cannot demand total dependence. We should learn to be satisfied with a 'limited level of dependence conditioned upon the overall health of our relationships,' but never total dependence. We should learn to accept this reality gracefully without making too much fuss or noise about it.

Advocating independence in relationships might also appear inconsistent with the objective of 'enforcing teamwork.'

However, 'teamwork' is an objective negotiation process between two independent partners, and not a sign of partners' dependence on each other.

Nonetheless, the options are clear: We could either keep looking for magical compromises, or agree on a set of principles that best fits the mentality of couples in modern societies. These principles, of course, lean toward partners' higher independence. The new trends indicate that couples consider independence their most urgent personal need, and give it the highest priority in their relationships too. Therefore, based on the strong trends evident in society, we can say that:

"Since we humans are usually unable to respond to the rotating demands of our partners for independence and dependence, we must adopt a relationship model to deal with the situation consistently. The rising social fervour for independence suggests that, as a rule, couples should start with a relationship model that has the highest potential for guaranteeing partners' independence. Accordingly, partners should reduce their expectations from relationships in terms of satisfying their dependence needs as well."

Whether we like it or not, it is now time to adjust our assumptions about the conflicting needs of partners for both dependence and independence. It is time to stop the negative impact of these useless struggles on relationships. These facts should be clear to couples at the outset before getting married. This is necessary because, nowadays, the idea of 'dependence' has been losing its practicality in relationships. Therefore, couples must think through and plan their relationships based on the assumption that they must remain independent in all respects regardless of the outcome of their relationships. Let us hope partners learn teamwork and compromise, too, to make their relationships manageable. However, starting on the wrong foot, i.e., hoping that their need for dependency can be satisfied in a relationship, is simply opening the door for major disappointments.

The relationship models (success factors) discussed in Part III place the highest emphasis on partners' degree of independence. In fact, this principle would provide the basis for setting all the other expectations defined in Table 3.1. Our personal need for independence has become the locus of all other relationship expectations. Our urge for independence has affected all the expectations we traditionally had from relationships, especially financial security, i.e., the expectation number 3.

As noted before, the worst case is when a partner is really craving security and dependence upon his/her partner, but keeps playing the role of an independent person forcefully, while also nagging about his/her partner's insensitivity. He/she does not admit that he/she is the one restricting his/her partner's ability to feel his/her need for dependence. He/she does not realize that his/her sudden need for attention (and expecting his/her partner to sense it automatically too) is frustrating his/her partner.

3. Financial Security is a rather obsolete concept, although many relationships are still based on one member of the family being the main breadwinner. The point is that financial security is no longer an automatic arrangement like the old times. People are not getting into relationships for the sake of financial security anymore. Or at least they should not when society is revolving around 'independence.' Now, financial security in relationships, when it happens, is mainly by accident or some kind of agreement between partners. It is an exception, not an expectation. Financial security is no longer a norm, but rather a possible by-product of being in a relationship and only in the spirit of teamwork.

Simply, partners nowadays (must) get into relationships with confidence in their abilities to support themselves financially if their relationships do not work out. It seems silly nowadays to envision that couples get into relationships for financial security. In the past it worked. However, this concept feels increasingly more incongruent with the values of equality, which is so seriously pursued, particularly by women. Obviously, many couples would continue to prefer dependency on their partners. It would be difficult to draw the lines so rigidly (about independence). However, here we are talking about *setting mindsets* that are realistic and congruent with other aspects of our desires. Relationships would continue to fail because of so many factors. Only one of them would be partners' reluctance to be self-sufficient and competent, and hoping that a relationship would rectify their financial insecurity.

Nowadays, partners should somehow understand and agree on the mechanism of their household finance before they commit themselves to a relationship. Accordingly, the more relevant topic that has emerged is 'financial control' and not 'financial security.'

In terms of financial control, also, the trend is changing. In the recent past, financial control referred to situations where one or both partners insisted on (or fought about) controlling the whole financial affair, even if the other partner made all the money. Even though both partners rather discussed some aspects of financial decisions, usually one partner ended up being in control of financial issues and bank accounts (although they usually shared the accounts). Nowadays, partners must be responsible for their own share of the pie, whether they have earned it themselves or is allotted to them through some type of family budget. Financial autonomy is now an essential factor that partners must discuss and plan at the outset. Therefore, the phrase 'Financial Control' is now more appropriately referring to the fact that each partner should keep financial control over his/her own financial affair. The other partner should not expect otherwise. The matter of sharing income, and any type of joint investments, is a reasonable arrangement when it is done voluntarily and through cooperation and teamwork, but never as an expectation anymore.

Those of us who are still in the transition process must over-haul our mentality.

4. Communication: This is still a major expectation from re-lationships. Effective communication is obviously the essence of successful relationships, especially for enforcing teamwork. However, many good relationships are ruined nowadays due to simple misperceptions and miscommunications. Partners' oversensitivity, arrogance, and false pride usually obstruct even common dialogues. Effective communication is also es-sential for implementing a process of hassle-free separation when necessary. Instead of spending time and money on law-yers, a prenuptial contract, as well as partners' objectivity, can enhance communication when separation seems inevitable. Nonetheless, effective communication is the most difficult expectation from relationships, because most often partners are not properly trained to communicate, or because retaliation and Ego make the process extremely hard to manage.

5. Compassion: Our ability to give and receive compassion is a direct function of our humanness and humility, which are becoming scarcer every year. Compassion depends on how good and enlightened a person is. Expecting compassion in relationships is a logical expectation. However, in reality it seldom materializes at the desired level. This is because eve-rybody seeks more compassion every day while the number of humble and patient people in society is shrinking. Our superfi-cial gestures of compassion, mostly through role-playing or even submission, cannot fill the gap for real compassion ei-ther. People often detect our hypocrisy and resent it, mostly because we cannot play a natural role. Therefore, it is wise to set our expectations rather low for receiving real compassion in relationships nowadays. But if relationships cannot fulfil our thirst for compassion, the question is whether we can fill this gap in our lives in some other way? Need for compassion is too strong and urgent to ignore, after all. The answer is that we may in fact learn to play a major role personally in this matter, as will be suggested shortly.

The problem is that we always crave sympathy, but have difficulty expressing it ourselves. Often we feel that our partners' needs are too superfluous and selfish. It is demanded too often or the nature of their expectations seems unreasonable to us. Sympathizing sincerely is difficult, anyway, even when we feel that our partners' need for compassion is genuine. This is because most humans are inherently more selfish than compassionate. Overall, people's need for sympathy is tremendously higher than we, as humans, are capable of delivering, especially in the new era. Therefore, the supply and demand for compassion are drastically unbalanced in societies and across the nations. Yet, instead of understanding this general shortfall of human nature, we take the matter personally and turn against our partners when they cannot give us as much compassion as we seek. We do not notice our own inability to offer genuine sympathy often enough, but we are needy for it so relentlessly.

Modern life complexity is creating additional mayhem and stress for everybody. Accordingly, demand for sympathy has increased astronomically. This is happening at the time when people are becoming more egotistical, impatient, and mentally unprepared (because of their own problems and stress) to provide sympathy to others. A person under constant pressure at work and from life issues is too preoccupied and exhausted to provide empathy to others, including his/her spouse. This is especially true if his/her partner's demands are only for satisfying her/his deficiency need for attention. Partners are playing enough games outside the house. And then expecting them to use their exhausted brain to play similar games at home is simply impractical. Despite this obviously persistent problem, marriage counsellors keep advocating artificial means of expressing compassion in order to satiate the needs of partners.

Besides the points expressed above, the problem with this approach is that it would not be perceived genuine often enough by the receiver, and the giver loses the patience and interest to play games. Nevertheless, compassion must be viewed in two dimensions as explained in the next two paragraphs.

On the one hand, couples should realize that expecting sympathy is unrealistic in a modern society where the supply and demand for compassion are unbalanced—mostly due to inherent human nature. Stress and depression have simply made us vulnerable and too needy for sympathy, but there is nobody out there to give it to us. So, expecting it on a regular basis is both selfish and a definite cause for disappointment. The bottom line is that everybody is alone in this world—an old saying that makes more sense every day as we constantly adopt more egotistical values and individualism. Therefore, we must define our lives personally and live it the best way we can within the stressful routines of modern society. Sympathy and compassion would be exchanged naturally when people are capable and ready to express it. However, it would lead to further alienation and resistance if it is demanded or even perceived as an expectation. Receiving sympathy (and giving it) is a fringe benefit and not a right. Exchanging compassion is nice and must be encouraged and appreciated. However, its inadequacy must not cause additional stress in relationships. Our partners might not be good in expressing compassion even if they genuinely mean to provide it. Conversely, learning to mimic compassion by reading a few books or attending seminars would never make people more compassionate. If we are looking for phony compliments to satisfy our need for compassion, we will never reach satisfaction in relationships. We just keep asking for more love to feed our addiction.

On the other hand, compassion is a reasonable expectation from relationships—with a major reservation in terms of its nature and source. A more realistic definition for compassion nowadays should mostly emphasize on our personal ability to generate it instead of craving it. The best way to achieve this is by becoming a better person and supplying more compassion to others than demanding it. We must realize that we should expect compassion only if we are good at generating it ourselves. Just needing something does not give us an entitlement to get it. The irony is that the more we learn to give compassion sincerely, the more we receive it from others naturally, and the less we feel the need for phony sympathies. By learning to become a compassionate person truly, we become self-sufficient largely and get a lot in return too. Therefore, in a sense, we can generate the compassion that we need personally. Only this mentality can reduce our depression and dependence on psychiatrists to manage our lives. Need for compassion is too strong and urgent to ignore, after all.

6. Companionship: This is an automatic outcome of relationships, but we do not quite know its meaning or the means of benefiting from this basic privilege of relationships. Instead, we alienate our partners quickly based on our misperceptions and egoism. Furthermore, our initial perceptions about our companion usually prove to be erroneous before long.

We all prefer to have a companion, and relationships provide this chance, but the question is whether we prefer a lousy companion to loneliness. Conversely, finding an ideal companion is a matter of luck and usually a doomed expectation too. We all seek high-quality companions to get love and compassion. A companion must be like this or that, we imagine, while we strive to satisfy our need for love. In all, we have no proper education about the purpose and process of companionship. So, the comments made before about the supply and demand for compassion and love, apply to companionship too.

The main trick for enjoying our companions realistically is to learn the means of relating, as explained in Chapter Ten.

7. Teamwork: Couples' ability for teamwork is a major requirement for relationships. As we insist on more independence and individualism, the need for teamwork becomes greater in order to keep our big Egos under a leash. Obviously, for teamwork, partners must have some genuine qualities, including modesty and objectivity. Yet, people's *obsession for individualism* hinders *modesty* nowadays. Therefore, finding partners of such quality and implementing teamwork in relationships would be a major challenge. Nonetheless, teamwork is an absolute necessity.

For managing the 'relationship needs' and responding to at least some of our partners' personal needs, we must commit ourselves to teamwork and learn about the means of compromising. The urgency for teamwork is not still appreciated, since couples consider it a threat to their independence and authority. However, teamwork is the only tool available to couples to coordinate and monitor the manner of satisfying their relationships' needs. Thus, it should become a major expectation soon, with some training to go along with it. The methods of family teamwork must be developed soon too.

8. Love: Love can make couples' communication smoother and more effective. It also helps them satisfy their need for compassion. However, love does not qualify as a legitimate expectation from relationships, due to its illusive nature. We all like to taste love at least for starting a relationship, and love is a good gauge for measuring the degree of partners' attraction and success in satisfying their sexual need. However, we should not consider love a reliable factor to keep partners together. Love is not an objective measure for assessing relationships either. The reason is obvious. When we express love, we are influenced by a perception of Selfless love (SLove) while we are driven mostly by our Ego and love deficiency (ELove). We all have this spiritual need, SLove, to love someone or something passionately. When we meet a person who can stir this feeling in us, we consume ourselves with a perception of SLove. This individual becomes a mirage that satiates our need for SLove. At the same time, our need for ELove (ego-ridden deficiency love) further encourages us to identify this person as our soul mate. We are suddenly in love. This is great for bringing couples together. However, true SLove happens only rarely and only when partners are need-less and enlightened persons. Therefore, our perception of SLove is only a transitory 'perception' and not a reality. ELove, on the other hand, is an absolute reality and not a per-ception. Therefore, ELove continues to place more demands on partners every day, because its only purpose is to feed part-ners' selfish need for attention. It creates possessiveness, jeal-ousy, and frustration.

Let us use MLove as a term to signify a sense of civilized, tactful expression of love. It helps us express our unexagger-ated emotions and sweeten our relationships. Thus, maybe MLove should be listed as an expectation from relationships, with some reservation. The reservation relates to the nature of MLove, because it is not genuine enough to count on its con-tinual effectiveness. MLove contains role-playing and it lacks authenticity at some degree. Its effect depends on the strength of a person's talent for playing his role naturally. Not every-body can be good at it. On the other hand, MLove can help a lot to keep romance alive in relationships.

Many radical ideas have been proposed in this book. They make the nature of our relationships appear too dry and imper-sonal. This picture of pessimism might prove to be the reality that we must eventually face based on the values and culture we are embracing so fast, most often inadvertently. Therefore, MLove is a helpful and relatively realistic expectation to in-duce passion in relationships. It also reminds partners of the need to keep working on their relationship and communica-tion.

In general, however, love, as we express it so readily nowadays, is not going to help relationships. Therefore, **we must remove love as a legitimate expectation from relationships.** (Except for MLove.) We can use 'love' as a gauge for attraction and for facilitating communication, but not as a factor of relationship success.

The arguments presented before regarding 'compassion' apply here too. We all seek love too much but do not know how to give love. We think we do, but, for the reasons noted throughout this book, we are only assuming to know what love is and how we can offer it to others. Again, the supply and demand for love (all three kinds, e.g., SLove, ELove, and MLove) are unbalanced and causing undue pressure on our lives and society in general. We have become too needy for love since everything else in society is stressful. And we assume that by stating love to someone, he/she gains the power or expertise to provide the genuine sympathy we need to mitigate social pressures.

The notations SLove, ELove, and MLove mentioned above have the following definitions in this book:

- SLove (selfless love) is the purest kind of love we feel toward our children, Nature, and possibly for our artistic creations.
- ELove (egotistic love) reflects the selfish need for love and attention and is mostly a reflection of insecurity.
- MLove (model love) is the tactful expressions of love to show compassion and cope with social etiquette.

9. Trust: Discussion in Chapter Two showed why mistrust is becoming a general condition in relationships nowadays. However, partners should stop fussing about it and instead live with some level of it as long as the integrity of their relationship is not jeopardized. Total trust cannot be a legitimate expectation.

10. Happiness: We expect relationships and our partners to bring us happiness. We expect joy and tranquility as a result of finding a companion. Overall, neither our partners nor our relationships are capable of providing happiness. Whether we can find happiness in relationships or not depends on a large number of factors, but mainly our mental capacity to interpret, absorb, and reflect happiness. In all, happiness is more a subjective perception than a tangible commodity to expect from relationships. If anything, relationship environments are normally too complex and demanding to exert direct happiness. It is our responsibility and art to enjoy our companion and explore the merits of being in a relationship. Usually, if we are a happy person, we know how to generate our happiness within or without a relationship. The opposite is even truer. If we have no capacity for being happy, relationships normally make us unhappier. Therefore, in all cases, expecting happiness from our relationships or partners is unrealistic. Couples should accept that the only source of happiness that could be expected from relationships is the mere presence of a companion in their lives. If a partner's presence alone does not cause happiness automatically, the relationship has no other source of happiness to offer. Under this circumstance, the couple must either learn to relate (at least passively) or opt for separation, but not nagging and demanding love and happiness.

We usually think that relationships can bring us happiness because it can solve our personal problems. This is a false assumption and an unrealistic expectation too. In fact, this mentality is destroying relationships and further reducing its capacity to cause even a slight measure of peace and comfort. As a whole, expecting relationships to solve our problems is a damned expectation. A good relationship helps us mentally to deal with our personal problems more effectively, if we were smart and humble. A bad relationship, on the other hand, destroys our ability to even take care of our basic needs, let alone solve the complicated problems of life and the relationship needs itself. Judging by the statistics, more relationships fail than succeed. Therefore, instead of expecting relationships to solve our problems, we should expect and prepare ourselves to deal with the hardships of relationships and the high likelihood of separation. Relationships become the source of new problems instead of solving our existing problems. That is what this book, and the other books in this series are all about—trying to prepare the readers for the headaches of relationships.

Playing more roles and games to exert happiness would not work either. Although many experts advocate role-paying to make couples release their tensions and express the sources of their anxiety, this author believes that couples can decide about the viability of their relationships only by understanding the deep-rooted causes of relationship obstacles in the new era. Relying on the intelligence of partners to learn the sad truth about relationships works better than keeping them hopeful by playing some artificial roles. This is especially true when they are already under pressure mentally and physically. Role-playing causes more stress and frustration when partners feel the futility of their efforts deep down. Why they feel this way? From experience, we know that once the process of alienation between partners begins, it is almost impossible to return it to its initial state of moderate tranquility. The only thing that can save relationships is learning the truth about the real causes of problems, which often relate to partners' own irreparable idiosyncrasies.

11. Friendship: A good test of 'relationship success' is partners' ability to enhance their friendship. However, this idea has never been promoted as an expectation. Often couples actually prove their inability to be friends, but still insist naively to build a relationship. The main feature of successful friendships, which is missing in relationships, is that friends' limited expectations are set gradually and naturally without pressure or demand. Then even if those expectations are not fulfilled, they seldom argue or fight over them. They only moderate (realign) their own expectations to keep their friendship. They value their friendship so much they willingly reduce their expectations. This is indeed the strength of good friendships and a main reason for their success and longevity. This is exactly an opposite mentality we see in relationships. In relationships, couples set high expectations immediately and do not appreciate the value of what they have like the way friends do. In fact, couples keep increasing their demands and expectations, and nag all the time, too, until their relationship falls apart. Therefore, a new expectation that should be promoted and analysed more actively in relationships is partners' aptitude for friendship. A relationship should be expected to be based more on friendship than love.

12. Respect/Social Acceptance: As part of our struggle for equality, independence, and identity, couples nowadays demand total respect from their partners. This is in line with social trends and thus an absolutely acceptable expectation from relationships. However, partners should not only expect respect. Rather, they should really learn how to respect their partners despite their obvious idiosyncrasies and personality weaknesses.

Society gives a higher status to family than individuals. We personally value our relationships highly for many reasons, too, but mainly because we expect them to help us fit better within the society. This is an automatic by-product and expectation from relationships.

13. Personal Success: A relationship should facilitate partners' personal success and independence. There is a positive consequence for this seemingly selfish need of partners for personal success. That is, with the emphasis on the personal success, partners need only look for the appropriate relationship model that can best fulfil the range of their personal needs. Otherwise, they should not even bother getting into a relationship. After all, if partners feel successful and fulfilled individually, their relationship would be a success too. It makes total sense.

Partners' cooperation is expected to give them a higher chance for success in social and personal endeavours. Synergy and moral support are the expected benefits of companionship. In all, personal success is a reasonable and helpful criterion to include in the list of realistic relationship expectations. Unfortunately, in reality, the very sense of individualism and independence forces partners to compete with each other. Their unrelenting urges for recognition and showing off their independence and identity make them too arrogant at the cost of losing their relationship. Thus, couples must not only choose the right relationship model based on their personalities and need for achievement, but also keep their Egos under a leash.

14. Commitment: We have traditionally expected relationships to enforce some form of commitment for partners to stick together even when some aspects of their relationship are not ideal. Maybe 'commitment' was a useful tool in the past and even now. However, as a practical step, partners should begin to realize that nowadays the sense of commitment is vastly eroded by the need for individualism. Nowadays, couples insist on enjoying their lives at the highest level possible. They get out of their relationships sometimes even based on childish reasons or their perceptions of a better life with a different partner. The bottom line is that commitment can no longer be considered a reasonable expectation from relationships in the new era. Period.

15. Longevity: The above arguments used for 'commitment' apply to longevity too. It was a practical expectation in the past but not anymore. Points 2 and 7 above (about Dependence and Teamwork) also explain why longevity erodes due to people's inability to balance their rising needs for independence and dependence.

Using the above analyses, and doing all the additions and deletions, the last column in Table 3.2 shows the updated list of realistic relationship expectations for the new era. Therefore, out of the seventeen general expectations from relationships, we can realistically consider only nine of them still relevant and practical in the new era, as marked by (X) in the right-hand-side column. In the following chapters, we will use this new set of expectations to develop a relationship framework and a set of relationship principles.

Table 3.2: The Updated List of Relationship Expectations

Type of Expectation	Delete Old	Add or Emphasize New	Sensible Expectations
1. Sex			X
2. Dependence	X		
3. Financial Security	X		
4. Communication		X	X
5. Compassion			X
6. Companionship			X
7. Teamwork		X	X
8. SLove	X		
9. ELove	X		
10. MLove		X	X
11. Trust	X		
12. Happiness	X		
13. Friendship		X	X
14. Respect-Social acceptance		X	X
15. Personal Success		X	X
16. Commitment	X		
17. Longevity	X		

In the following chapters, we will use this new set of expectations to develop a relationship framework and a set of relationship principles. Reducing our expectations from relationships seems like a major radical idea that partners must consider and implement along with many other radical solutions noted in

Chapter Eight. Developing this new mentality is crucial, if we are truly serious about improving the state of relationships. Radical solutions are meant to facilitate partners' ability to distinguish their realistic expectations from unrealistic one in line with new social values. The main goal is to introduce innovative social mechanisms that support the process of partners' mental adjustment.

Chapter Four
Identifying Relationship Needs

An ideal relationship can *potentially* cover many of our basic, medium, and high-level needs. This is exactly why we naively *perceive* 'relationship needs' as a natural extension of our 'personal needs.' This confusion is the symptom of our phony social values making us too needy and desperate. However, placing such an extreme demand on relationships, to fulfil so many of our personal needs at all levels, is unrealistic. Especially, our new social order—where everybody seeks individualism so obsessively—cannot deal with this huge demand. Furthermore, our misperception about the role of love, as the main factor for the success of relationships, deters our grasp of relationship needs, while it makes us increase our demands on our relationships even more.

Some other implications are important to notice as well. First, the above facts emphasize the inherent significance of having a good companion. An ideal companion can seemingly solve almost all of our problems and needs. Second, this psychological significance (and urgency) suggests that companionship must be viewed as a *basic* personal need, and not merely an extension of social (medium range) need. This important viewpoint, and its impact on relationships, will be elaborated further in Chapter Eleven.

Nevertheless, 'relationship needs' must supersede our 'personal needs' if we are really interested in the health of our relationships. We should learn to look at the bigger picture and stop fussing about our long list of artificial personal needs, especially love and trust. We must find ways of fulfilling our personal needs independently so that the burden on relationships is reduced.

We witness the sad facts about relationships, feel the heavy toll this situation is taking on our health, and still continue with our present approaches and mentality. Why are we, as partners in this common cause, incapable of agreeing on a solution? Why do we actually sabotage the process of achieving our common goal, i.e., a manageable relationship, by humiliating and traumatizing our partners? Is it because we soon get tired of a relationship we had so eagerly tried to get into? Is it because partners' personal needs suffocate their relationship? Are our personal idiosyncrasies and insecurities getting out of control? Are too many philosophical slogans obscuring our sense of reality? Is our Ego and impatience stopping us from reaching a decent compromise? Is our sense of romanticism preventing us from assessing relationship hurdles practically before marriage? Are not we intelligent enough? Are we hoping for miracles to save our relationships instead of relying on proper principles to keep it together? Or is our legal system, which must strengthen the foundation of family life, in fact hurting the situation? The answer is: All of the above.

Therefore, the first step is to find those *specific needs of relationships* that can bring some form of harmony into relationships. The second step is to enhance partners' willingness and patience to learn these needs. They should understand how relationship needs may clash with their personal needs. Furthermore, they must curb their Egos to stay objective. Many issues must be sorted out to make a relationship work, eh? Absolutely! Nonetheless, we must learn to view 'relationships' as a unique entity with specific needs, which are totally different from the conflicting needs of the partners in it. It is a pity that our educational systems, especially at senior high school, do not devote a good portion of its required curriculum to this essential real life subject.

Tables 4.1 and 4.2 reflect the result of discussions in the previous chapter and summarized in Table 3.2. Relationship needs can be developed around the list of valid relationship expectations (Table 4.1). Fulfilling these needs enhances the favorability of relationships. This list is not necessarily an ultimate or complete list of relationship needs or success factors for relationships. Yet, it provides a solid platform as a working platform. The more favourable the noted factors in Table 4.1, the more successful a relationship would be. Many other factors could be identified and added to Table 4.1 later by scholars and researchers.

Table 4.1 **Realistic Relationship** **Expectations**	**Table 4.2** **Unrealistic Relationship** **Expectations**
1. Sex 2. Communication 3. Compassion 4. Companionship 5. Teamwork 6. MLove 7. Friendship 8. Respect -Social acceptance 9. Personal Success	1. Dependence 2. Security 3. SLove 4. ELove 5. Trust 6. Happiness 7. Commitment 8. Longevity

Of course, the unrealistic expectations listed in Table 4.2 might materialize in some relationships automatically. However, they should be taken as fringe benefits of that particular relationship. The point is that couples must not start a relationship based on these invalid expectations, as they hardly materialize and last in relationships. It does not mean that their relationship is abnormal when they face the reality. Fulfilling the expectations in Table 4.1 is a major success by itself. With this mindset, partners would not blame each other for unfulfilled expectations or fuss too much about them.

The irony is that if couples fulfil the expectations listed in Table 4.1 effectively, the ones in Table 4.2 would most likely be fulfilled automatically as well. They evolve gradually in their relationships based on partners' maturity. Once partners learn to live in peace with each other, love, happiness, and longevity would follow. But not if they keep insisting on the invalid expectations in Table 4.2. Actually, pressing for the items in Table 4.2 hinders the fulfilment of the moderate expectations in Table 4.1, and the relationship collapses under all the pressures quickly. Enjoying someone's companionship and basic compassion should suffice without partners going overboard. That type of arrangement would prove quite fulfilling, anyway, while couples' invalid expectations do not distract them from the main objectives of relationships. Yet, Ego and related emotions prevent people from staying content with a more realistic set of expectations. It looks bizarre when sometimes a partner starts to hate his/her partner and retaliates because he/she feels that his/her partner does not love him/her enough. The question is how an individual's own love turns into hatred because his/her partner cannot respond to his/her love. What kind of love he/ she had for his/her partner, anyway?

Relationship Objectives

Strangely, most of us have never learned about the real purposes of relationships. Instead, we trust our imagination and Ego to define them for us. Thus, we often fail. The realistic objectives of relationships, however, are only the ones listed in Table 4.1 and discussed in Chapter Three. In fact, relationship needs and objectives are almost identical. In ideal, mature relationships, the items in Table 4.2 turn into complementary objectives for those lucky couples.

The most important point, however, is that beyond these general objectives for relationships, the ultimate objective is to help couples face life's hardships together and reduce each other's burdens. Relationships could bring love and happiness to couples, too, but not as a main objective. The lack of adequate love or happiness in one's life is often only due to our exaggerated expectations from life and relationships as well as personal deficiencies. The reason for so many relationship failures nowadays is that our present mentality is set erroneously and we have no true grasp of relationship objectives, especially the ultimate purpose of making life just a bit more endurable for partners. That is all!

Couples' Responsibilities

Although we must view relationships as an independent entity, the onus is on partners to keep it functional, in the same manner that business partners and management should fulfil many responsibilities in order to keep their business together. Thus, 'Relationship Needs' and objectives refers to all the right things that partners must do for keeping their relationship healthy. Accordingly, Table 4.3 provides the list of 'Relationship Needs', which merely shows Couples' Responsibilities for satisfying the relationship expectations and objectives listed in Table 4.1 and making their relationships successful:

Table 4.3: Relationship Needs for the New Era
(Partners' Responsibilities for Building a Successful Relationship)

1. Relationship needs consist of the specific responsibilities that partners must carry on to fulfil the sensible expectations in Table 4.1 and achieve relationships' main objectives, all for giving their relationship a good chance for success.
2. Accordingly, Relationship Needs, Relationship Objectives, Partners' Responsibilities, and Success Factors have the

same (interrelated) implications, according to the points outlined in this Table.

3. Partners view their relationship as an independent entity (R-entity) that has specific needs, which are different from their personal needs.

4. Partners realize their responsibilities for fulfilling these unique Relationship Needs, as listed here, instead of relying on (and expecting) their relationship to satisfy their personal needs.

5. Partners distinguish their realistic expectations from unrealistic ones. Thus, they discuss and agree on focusing only on the realistic expectations from their relationship.

6. Partners give their relationship needs the highest priority as a sacred foundation for building a friendly environment free from dogmatism and pressures.

7. Partners keep their expectations within the boundary pinpointed in Table 4.1.

8. Partners know the repercussions of pushing the expectations in Table 4.2.

9. Partners are attracted to each other with good chemistry, both emotionally and intellectually.

10. Partners have chosen a relationship model suitable for their personalities. Relationship Models are discussed in Part III. Mainly, the purpose of relationship models is to set partners' means of relating straight. The objective is to maintain a balance between the levels of dependence and independence each partner needs. This balance must also make sense nowadays for relationships. Choosing the right relationship model that can best facilitate partners' communication and agreeing on that at the outset is very important. Obviously, the smart thing nowadays is to judge the degree of dependability of partners and the practical level of dependence based on partners' long-term behaviour and actions and not their words. People simply cannot deliver on their promises

because of the limitations in their own lives and psyches, and not necessarily out of malice or spite.

11. Partners maintain a high degree of personal integrity when dealing with each other.

12. Partners are mentally prepared to leave their relationship peacefully when reconciliation is not possible.

13. Partners adhere to teamwork, instead of retaliation, for convincing each other about something.

14. Partners are tactful, mature, forgiving, patient, and mentally stable.

15. Partners do not play games with each other.

16. Partners do not need, nor rely on, government or religion to regulate and run their relationship.

17. Partners have signed a contract at the outset to govern financial and other aspects of their relationship, especially during separation.

18. Partners consider separation a normal expectation in the new era.

19. Partners believe in terminating their relationships civilly if necessary.

20. Partners measure and discuss the state of their relationship regularly.

21. Partners remain independent financially and emotionally within the requirements of their relationship model, while they cooperate for drawing proper family plans and budges as well.

22. Partners know that, beyond people's *instinctual urge,* three other reasons make them seek independence in the new era: (1) they have become too obsessed with the idea of individualism and asserting their identity, (2) just for the sake of coping with social norms and be accepted, and (3) they eventually learn they cannot depend on others.

23. Partners understand that the main purpose of choosing a relationship model is to help them relate more effectively and handle many personal inner conflicts that arise from being

in a relationship. They realize that each partner should deal with his/her dilemma of dependence versus independence personally, as explained in the following three distinct ways:

- He/she should initially try to establish his/her realistic needs for dependence and independence, based on his/her personality alone, without taking into consideration any compromises necessary for being in any serious relationship with a partner. The idea is to establish one's true temperament and needs regardless of social pressures for independence or the level of compromise needed in a relationship.

- He/she should establish the levels of independency/ dependency that he/she can envision for his/her partner. Usually people dislike partners who seek too much independence. However, more crucial than this case is when a person is unprepared (perhaps psychologically) or unwilling to be responsible for a partner who requires too much dependence (emotionally or financially). Thus, he/she should figure out his/her potential partner's inclination for dependence/independence realistically before committing him/herself to any particular relationship model.

- Together with his/her potential partner, they should establish the kind of dependency/independency balance they require in their relationship. This balance should fit the other two above decisions that each partner must make personally, then they choose the right relationship model.

24. Partners can relate rather actively, regardless of the relationship model (level of independence) they have chosen.

25. Partners have compatible lifestyles and preferences.

26. Partners stay within the boundaries set by their relationship model.

27. Partners pursue a self-awareness routine to detect their personal idiosyncrasies that might damage their relationship.

28. Partners pursue a path of self-awareness also for enhancing their sense of self-reliance, individualism, Self, SLove, and personal search for self-fulfilment and compassion.

29. Partners know the meaning and repercussions of egotistical demands for love and attention. They know how to depend on Mlove, respect, and courtesy to spread a civilized sense of love and cooperation between them. They also know the meaning and implications of ELove, MLove, and SLove.

30. Partners grasp and negate the problems of misperceptions that confuse and hinder their communication. Misperceptions have various natures, including the ones mentioned in # 31 below. Generally, however, they result from partners' carelessness, oversensitivity, or impatience.

31. Partners know how everybody's personality is shaped and controlled by forces beyond their control. Two big misperceptions in relationships are that i) our partners are in control of their personalities and ii) they can change themselves easily. Thus, we rush to retaliate in our own ways in order to teach them a lesson. We ignore the fact that retaliations only add more barriers for couples to assess the viability of their relationships objectively.

32. Partners understand the inherent flaws of human nature and how they contaminate relationships.

33. Partners do not criticize each other's idiosyncrasies constantly.

34. Partners do not try to change each other or push their lifestyles on each other.

35. Partners strive sincerely to develop trust and dependence between them, but do not make an issue about the overall level of trust and dependence in their relationship.

36. Partners do not try to manipulate, control, or intimidate each other.

37. Partners know how to maintain good communication between them.

38. Partners enjoy having sex together and do not withdraw this basic need for retaliation and blackmail.
39. Partners run their household and family affairs mostly through teamwork.
40. Partners are compassionate and know how to show compassion through MLove.
41. Partners are good friends. They know the rules, boundaries, and benefits of friendship and stick to them.
42. Partners know that people's (including their partner's) idiosyncrasies limit their abilities to perceive and behave in an ideal manner. They use this knowledge to enhance their own compassion and patience in their relationship.
43. Partners respect each other despite their partner's irritating idiosyncrasies.
44. Partners are capable of promoting each other's needs for independence and pursuing their social ambitions.
45. Partners can support each other in pursuing their personal goals.
46. Partners are aware how their imposing personality aspects (e.g., Ego, Model, and Self) interfere during their encounters and watch their effects closely.
47. Partners know the concept and components of the Relationship Framework (as discussed in Part II).
48. Partners adopt the Relationship Framework and follow its guidelines actively.
49. Partners know, and actively follow a reliable set of relationship principles, like the ones suggested in Chapter Seven. They use these principles to always stay objective in their relationship and minimize the chances of anger and Ego tainting their judgment and decisions.
50. Partners seek mediation and consultation when disagreements arise.

PART II

Relationship Framework

Chapter Five

The Transition

Let us hope readers agree by now that we need a relationship framework to deal with the sad realities noted in Part I. Nevertheless, relationships will continue to go through a long, torturous transition in the 21st century with unpredictable outcome. We have the option of making this transition smoother toward a more thoughtful and acceptable relationship environment or just wait and let it happen through chaos, which would surely raise social disorder and stress too. The future of family and social health is in great jeopardy. And the outcome depends on our success to revamp our mindsets, develop a modern relationship framework, and introduce a bunch of radical social mechanisms compatible with couples' new lifestyles and drive for individualism.

Of course, developing and propagating a relationship framework would be a difficult task. Even defining its parameters would be gruelling since such a framework must be quite flexible to accommodate a large variety of couples' personalities. Furthermore, it must be justifiable as a practical approach to relationships with valid objectives. It must make sense to people around the world, especially to those living in progressive societies. It sounds like an impossible job, and the author is the first person to admit that. Yet all these hurdles can be conquered easily if only we change our mentality about relationships and see the need for a framework.

The ideal would have been to bring all the effective ideas that relationships experts are using nowadays together into one comprehensive, easy to understand document. The fact that we cannot do this easily simply proves that the ideas that scholars and marriage counsellors suggest to couples presently are ineffective and not universally acceptable.

Anyway, the simple fact remains that without a framework, the state of relationships would deteriorate beyond control very soon. It will reach a highly explosive and unmanageable level. Sooner or later, we will be forced to acknowledge that some kind of a framework is needed, so that we can assess and manage our relationships more objectively. So, we might as well get serious now. If we begin working on it now, we may have a reasonably practical framework in place within the next few decades or so. However, we would all benefit from this work in progress a great deal immediately, as soon as we adopt a new mentality about relationships. We must merely believe in the need for such a framework and then continue to work on its development seriously and systematically. The objectives of the relationship framework are discussed in the remainder of this chapter and then the benefits and means of this development are explained in the future chapters.

Objectives of a Relationship Framework

The main objectives of a relationship framework are to:

A. Enforce teamwork.
B. Bring objectivity back into relationships.
C. Increase the effectiveness of communications.
D. Reduce partners' expectations from relationships as much as necessary in order to create the right balance between their personal needs and the relationship needs.

E. Overhaul individuals' mentality and social mechanisms regarding relationships.

Discussing the merits and objectives of a relationship framework without knowing what a 'relationship framework' looks like might annoy some readers. So, a couple of points must be made in advance. First, although a preliminary format for a relationship framework will be suggested in the following chapters, developing its final form is not a task for this book. It will take many years before such a framework can be fully developed. Second, a relationship framework has many components, as discussed in Chapter Six. It is better to define these components first and then let the framework evolve by itself through these discussions. At least, this is the approach taken in this book. Nonetheless, convincing the readers about the *need* for a relationship framework—*why* and *how* it can help couples—is the most important task. Modifying people's mentality about relationships is the most important step. Therefore, this chapter will provide more details about the objectives of a relationship framework and then the following chapters will explain its format, components, principles, and characteristics.

Objective A: To enforce teamwork

Teamwork is not a revolutionary idea or a concept forgotten by couples. But knowing about teamwork and actually being committed to it, as the only solution for relationships, are two different things. Commitment to teamwork is, in particular, difficult while couples strive so obsessively for individualism and independence. Indeed, partners often perceive teamwork and individualism as two contradictory concepts. They often perceive their 'compromising' an infringement on their individualism. Their partners' suggestions come across as a deliberate opposition or an intrusion of their independence. This is how our Egos regularly operate. Therefore, a relationship framework must somehow overcome all these obstacles and prove the merits of real teamwork. The challenge is to invent the means of enforcing teamwork principles without threatening partners' individuality. The radical solutions explained in Chapter Eight would accomplish this objective largely, as partners would find it to their advantage to participate in teamwork naturally.

A major hurdle nowadays is that couples often do not know the meaning of compromise, or the method or timing to make one. Sometimes partners compromise just to show their sense of cooperation. They usually do this at the wrong time and for the wrong reasons. For example, a person is seeking his/her partner's objective and honest opinion to make the best decision together, but his/her partner simply agrees with him/her carelessly or maybe even callously. This partner is unaware of, or ignores, the process of reaching a compromise. He/she only pretends to do it just to show his/her cooperation, or simply because he/she has no guts to take the risk of expressing his/her opinion, e.g., about certain investment. And then this same partner makes a big fuss if the outcome of that decision (or compromise) turns out unsatisfactory. He/she tries to dissociate him/herself from the wrong decision. He/she declares his/her initial input only a simple gesture of support, and not a real consent. In all, partners often lose the opportunity of benefiting from each other's wisdom because they are incapable of discussing the merits and demerits of their plans calmly through teamwork. Other times, couples compromise simply because their partners are showing a lot of sensitivity (or resistance) toward a specific suggestion just out of spite or narrow-mindedness. Therefore, one partner gives in because reasoning stops working.

The ever-increasing need for individuality is a given fact in relationships. Accordingly, teamwork is facing the highest level of resistance by partners, due to their obsession for some imaginary sense of independence. They do not realize that teamwork is actually the only tool that can guarantee their independence, not arguments and retaliations. Enforcing such mentality in relationships would not be easy. And that is exactly why 'teamwork' is a main parameter of a relationship framework. It will take many decades for couples to change their mindsets and accept teamwork as a major requirement for maintaining both their independence and relationships. Yet, it must happen eventually to minimize havoc in relationships.

Obviously, there is no need to emphasize on the merits of teamwork in any environment. Rather, the idea is to stress that, for the mere reason that individuality is becoming the most important requirement of relationships, creating new methods of teamwork is imperative more than ever nowadays. New methods of teamwork might depend on a variety of tools, including a simple agreement about sharing family responsibilities and finances and sticking to the plan.

Another role of teamwork is to keep the balance between partners' personal needs and relationship needs, according to the relationship model they have chosen. It will be explained, in the future chapters, why couples' expectations from relationships must be reduced in order to exert a balance between their personal needs and relationship needs. To maintain this balance, and stay within the boundaries of their chosen relationship model, more teamwork is required.

Still another role of teamwork would be to abolish the need for equality struggles. People's misperceptions about equality (for causing major relationship conundrums) were discussed on page 24. Once partners learn to focus on teamwork, their obsession for *equality* subsides. Instead of depending on equality, or superiority, the success of relationships would be measured only by the smooth operation and outcome of teamwork—not the level of one partner's influence over the other.

Indeed, the strength of teamwork lies on its emphasis on partners' independence and objectivity. Their independent (yet objective) opinions are needed for important decisions of the family. This is more in line with the trend in society to promote individualism. Yet, it also gives partners a chance to use their unique expertise for the benefit of their relationship without being constantly second-guessed by their partners. In teamwork, partners' roles are clear. This is contrary to the existing approach where partners are confused or depressed about their roles because they are mostly preoccupied by equality games. It is indeed too difficult to understand the equality rules, since we have not yet established the objectives and means of *family equality*. Equality, and measuring it, remains at best ambiguous and arbitrary. It lives only in people's imaginations and it manifests in the form of immature games of resistance and confrontation with no definite purpose or guideline.

Everybody is paranoid about fairness these days. Therefore, the relationship framework should replace the need for couples' constant struggle for equality. By insisting on *equality* in all aspects of relationships, couples are wasting energy on measuring every activity or incident subjectively instead of focusing on teamwork objectively. The flexibility of a universal framework could replace the rigidity of equality approach.

Usually relationships thrive when couples adopt complementary roles while giving each other room to act independently. They do not need to fight for inequality, unfairness, lack of independence, etc. A relationship framework would facilitate both teamwork and partners' independence. While men and women have the same rights and acknowledge each other's contributions, they need not share the same tasks and roles to ensure equality. This is an obvious concept, but in reality couples waste a lot of energy nowadays, consciously or subconsciously, on measuring the difficulty of various responsibilities and quarrelling about them. Presently, nobody knows enough about the mechanism of a reliable relationship framework, while only some imaginary notions about relationships confuse couples.

The best test of equality in terms of partners' decision making or sharing household affairs is to see how well those activities and processes fit within the guidelines of teamwork. If they do not fit, then they are biased, Ego driven, and futile. Conversely, understanding the guidelines of teamwork and implementing them in relationships would enhance partners' Self and Model at the expense Ego—thus more effective relationships. In all, teamwork guidelines would inherently ensure couples' fairer treatment of each other, which is the objective of equality struggles theoretically. By adhering to some basic guidelines for relationships (and teamwork), partners' rights would be best served in an environment built for coexistence. So the question is, if any standards can be invented what would they look like? We will tackle this question in the future chapters of this book.

Considering the power of teamwork, it is amazing how our Ego prevents Self and Model to play a more prominent role in relationships and make teamwork a more successful mechanism. Thus, an important objective of the relationship framework is to *enforce* teamwork. The format of the relationship framework is such that teamwork cannot be bypassed.

Objective B: To bring objectivity back into relationships

Objectivity has been eroded in relationships nowadays due to couples' rising Ego and expectations. Relationships are erroneously perceived as a mechanism to fulfil a large variety of partners' personal needs.

In the author's opinion, objectivity was more defined and achievable a few decades ago because relationship goals were limited, manageable, and better understood. Those objectives fell more in line with the traditional and instinctual needs of humans to cooperate for building a family. But now, with all the demands for love, compassion, independence, and extravagant lifestyles, relationships are burdened by a large collection of artificial expectations. In line with our personal obsession for more things and more affection, we have reduced the capacity of our relationships to be objective. Furthermore, partners have different ideas about the type and level of personal needs that their relationship should satisfy.

In all, couples' subjective perceptions of relationships and their unrealistic demands have made the task of managing relationships quite difficult for couples. Therefore, to reduce family clashes, we must somehow bring objectivity back into relationships by creating a practical relationship framework and viewing relationships as an independent entity separate from couples' personalities. Couples' personalities must not overwhelm their relationships constantly.

The new framework must help (and rather force) couples set their objectives and expectations from relationships more realistically. The framework could also provide couples with the opportunity of settling their conflicts objectively despite all the inevitable emotional episodes in relationships. Furthermore, the framework must identify a handful relationship models that can fit a large variety of individuals' personalities, while each model provides the fundamental advantages of being in a relationship. The ultimate goal is to minimize arguments about every task or issue and to reduce couples' urge for aggressive behaviour when they feel some kind of unfairness.

Relationships are supposed to create synergy when couples combine their resources, especially their brains, effectively. Often, however, the opposite happens when retaliations bring couples' lives to a halt. Instead of empowering each other, partners often compete and retaliate. A reason for conflicts in relationships is that couples keep arguing about the roles they would like to play, either independently or jointly. Each partner likes to set the rules for their relationship. This decision is often based on his/her rotating and abrupt preference to push his/her *need for independence*, (e.g., making investment or some family decisions alone), or *need for dependence*, (e.g., seeking support and attention). One objective of a relationship framework is to eliminate conflicts caused by these extreme need changes of partners or equality arguments. The modest guidelines of a framework could replace couples' arbitrary and emotional decision processes in relationships. Obviously, synergy is achieved better, usually, when partners work together to fulfil certain tasks or share decision-making needs of a relationship. However, synergy can be achieved also if couples support each other to perform their roles separately with real independence.

In recent decades, relationships' success is determined only by partners' feelings. Although the feelings and impressions of partners matter a lot, they do not reflect whether their relationship failed due to partners' exaggerated expectations, oversensitivity, or real lack of compatibility. Nowadays, we rely on partners to assess their relationship because there is no definition for a successful relationship. Two partners in a particular relationship might actually rate the success of their relationship quite differently. This is because they are biased and mostly act based on their raw emotions. Furthermore, this type of assessment lacks any basis to compare different relationships against one another and find universally agreeable anomalies. Couples' assessments of their own relationships would reveal one interesting fact, though: that most relationships are failures if we asked couples to rate it. This is because almost nobody is quite happy these days with his/her relationship. Seldom would both partners consider their relationship a success. Even then, they are probably using wrong or biased criteria for measuring its success.

Another reason for partners' lousy impressions of their relationships, and the overall loose definition for 'relationship success,' is that our expectations from relationships are growing too fast. This situation cannot continue forever. As noted repeatedly, relationship expectations are increasing due to the rampant increase in couples' personal needs and social push for extravagance. Everybody is imagining some phony life-style or ideals, which he/she imposes on their relationships too. This selfish attitude is raising the bar for relationship success beyond all reasonable limits. The list of relationship expectations has become larger than the sum of all the expectations that people have imitated from one another and the movies. That is, everybody likes to have everything that all other couples have in their relationships plus everything else that their imaginations tell them. Instead of measuring the success of relationships objectively, we let the selfishness and neediness of partners make this critical judgment. It is only their arrogance that is being measured then, and not the success of their relationship. Surely, this open-ended level of expectations from relationships cannot prevail forever. The faster these expectations rise, the less successful relationships become (appear to people).

With our rampant needs for things, sympathy, and security, we are placing a lot of pressure on society and limiting the chances of relationships to follow a practical path. And the impact of the failing relationships is depressing individuals and society as a whole, too, which then again stirs up people's mistrust, but also their urge for more compassion. This vicious cycle is feeding and forcing itself out of control. We must somehow deal with this situation before the time comes when everybody needs antidepressants in order to go through a day. We must redefine relationships as an independent entity with unique needs. We must agree that relationship expectations beyond some modest, humanistic level are whimsical and imposed by psychologically distressed and deprived people.

Couples should monitor the relationship needs (success factors) that were discussed in Part I. More importantly, however, they must learn to disallow superficial criteria (their subjective judgments) obscure their views of their relationships. It means no more imposing of their personal needs on their relationships and measuring their partners' compliance with their crooked expectations. Now, we need a *relationship framework* to create a balance between our personal needs and relationship needs.

Objective C: To increase communications effectiveness

Partners' communications have become too emotional, subjective, Ego driven, and destructive. This deficiency is obviously causing many relationship conflicts. And the situation will continue to worsen unless couples are given better tools for communicating and relating more effectively. The objective is to minimize the effect of partners' Egos during family discussions. This is a rather unrealistic expectation. However, a relationship framework might achieve this important task to some extent. It would give partners an opportunity to make their communications less egotistical and more goal-oriented. It would also reduce arguments altogether by giving partners more autonomy in a teamwork environment. We can never eliminate arguments and bad communications, especially when one or both partners are egotistical or mentally sick. However, for reasonably logical couples, a relationship framework provides enough guidelines for partners to negotiate within certain boundaries and thus minimize the chances of miscommunication.

A major flaw in our approach toward relationships is that we usually examine a relationship only when it is in trouble. Otherwise, it is taken for granted the way our ancestors did intuitively. Driven by our traditional mindset, we still assume (and expect) that relationships would continue to work smoothly as a routine social arrangement. However, then, relationships were defined by simple cultural rules and they remained inherently safe. In new societies, however, relationships are extremely vulnerable from day one, because a lot of complexities and expectations have complicated the interworking of relationships. Accordingly, partners cannot comprehend or respond to relationship needs intuitively. In fact, they cannot detect the real causes of relationship problems even when they attempt to explore them actively. Not even relationship experts and counsellors can help couples in most cases. The irony is that most often the problems are simply due to partners' naïveté about the purpose and potentials of relationships, as their criteria is gravely tainted by artificial values and imitation. Most relationships would have been considered acceptable if couples were not misled by phony lifestyles and misperceptions. For this reason alone, unfortunately, couples' struggle to salvage their relationships usually proves futile, despite all the efforts that partners and marriage counsellors put into them. Partners do not know how to communicate about the rising relationship conflicts in a timely and proper manner.

Objective D: Reduce our expectations from relationships

The fourth objective of a relationship framework is to keep partners' expectations low. They should reduce their expectations as much as necessary until a balance between their personal needs and relationship needs is created. They must understand and respect the set boundaries. Nowadays, we value our individuality and independence more than we value our relationships. However, at the same time, we have been placing more demands on relationships. For example, we expect our partners and relationships to bring us happiness and a lot of compassion. This is an unrealistic expectation, because the logic dictates that the more we seek independence, the less we like to depend on others, and the less we should expect from our relationships too. We must become more self-reliant to maintain our independence and individuality.

Couples must learn that personal needs and relationship needs are not the same or coincidental. Every relationship consists of two individuals with different personalities and perceptions. Thus, their conflicting personal needs cause relationship clashes. Especially, while both partners insist on individualism, the areas of common interest between them decline drastically. Each partner gives priority to his/her personal needs and his/her perceived expectations from a relationship. Therefore, they cannot comply with the particular needs of relationships, even if they knew what they were. At best, if they really wanted to be in this relationship, they must decide how to reduce their expectations from their relationship. In practice, however, it is hard to expect this kind of understanding and sacrifice, especially from young couples. Thus, a relationship framework is needed to do it for them, i.e., reconcile couples' personal needs with the relationship needs in a logical and proactive manner.

A useful relationship framework must have a flexible structure to somehow accommodate a large variety of personalities, while attempting to modify partners' perceptions of relationships too. Obviously, this framework would not fulfil all the personal needs and objectives of couples. It can fulfil only a bunch of global needs that are most commonly agreeable to the public. These global needs would not necessarily include enough personal needs of all couples, e.g., love or happiness. The relationship framework cannot bring happiness to partners. It only provides the right atmosphere for smart partners to find happiness individually first and then possibly in their relationship too. Couples thus learn that they cannot depend on their relationships to fulfil all their personal needs, especially happiness.

The relationship framework would be incapable of responding to partners' subjective preferences for their relationship. Yet, partners learn gradually that observing the general guidelines of a framework would potentially give their relationship a better chance to survive. They may not like all the features of this framework, but it would be better than arguing with their partners all the time or living alone. Since all relationships would be following the same guidelines, no one would feel oppressed in a particular relationship. They also know that going to a different relationship would not change the rules of the game. People would judge all relationships and their success based on couples' ability to adhere to the general guidelines of the relationship framework. Partners get into relationships with advance knowledge of the rules of the game. If they do not like the framework, they should not start a relationship, unless both partners agree to have a relationship arrangement outside this global framework. Therefore, couples would still have a choice to set their relationships outside the norms of a relationship framework if they desired to do so. However, for the majority of us, sticking to a general framework would prove more practical and effective in the long run.

A major purpose of developing a framework is to discuss and eliminate some of the existing misperceptions about relationships. Once we have a better appreciation of what does not work anymore in the new era, we can set out to create the new framework and a more practical mindset. In all, we must reduce our expectations from relationships drastically.

Objective E: To overhaul couples' mentality and social mechanisms

As evident from the discussions in this chapter, a great deal of soul searching and mental adjustments is needed in order to adapt our relationships to the new social framework. We need radical changes in our mentality, and we must change social mechanisms, especially the legal system, to fit our new personal needs and lifestyles. These topics, as well as some solutions, are discussed in Chapter Eight.

The Ultimate Objective of a Relationship Framework

The above noted objectives A through E are important steps needed for improving the state of relationships. However, it must be emphasized that the *ultimate* objective for developing the 'relationship framework and models' is to make as many relationships *manageable* as possible. Even imperfect relationships have some merits if only couples learn to relate (at least passively). Daydreaming about an ideal relationship is only a waste of our precious lives. We must, instead, control our imagination about the potentials and purposes of relationships and find mechanisms to manage them somehow. For this sacred objective, we need a relationship framework based on the values of our modern society.

The first step, of course, is to imagine and agree that: A relationship is an *independent* setting, and not a collection of partners' untamed expectations (from each other and their relationship). Then we can set out to develop a framework that defines and supports the properties and boundaries of this independent entity—relationships. The main assumption is that working from within this framework gives partners a better chance to relate. This implies that partners agree on the relationship needs listed in Table 4.3 and learn to follow some specific guidelines to *relate* to each other, instead of hoping for it to happen automatically or by a lifelong trial and error.

In the old times, relationships were not particularly important, understood, or perfect. Couples had simply come to terms with the limitations of relationships and did not jump out of them when they were not perfect. They had more tolerance naturally because their brains were not washed with some imaginary notions about relationships. They were not obsessed with love or an idealistic perception of relationships. But now everything has changed. Particularly, three clashing conditions are making life unbearable for everybody: 1) Relationships have become too complex, 2) we crave the opportunity of having a soul mate more than ever, and 3) we have become too demanding and arrogant but less patient. Our naïve perceptions are making life unbearable for everybody and the situation would get even worse if a solution is not found soon. We must review the real potentials of relationships in our present culture in order to cleanse our wild imaginations. It is crucial to realize that relationships are not capable of giving us all the niceties that have gradually turned into relationship expectations in recent decades. We have created only more deprivation for ourselves by our exaggerated perception of relationship potentials, especially in terms of bringing us happiness.

Obviously, we all need a companion with certain qualities and mutual attraction. The problem is not as much in finding him/her as it is in keeping them. In fact, people's traditional tolerance in relationships has been suddenly replaced by oversensitivity and edginess nowadays. The reasons behind people's chronic impatience are noted throughout this book. However, social stress, our increasing need for individualism, romanticism, loss of trust, and thirst for love and respect are to be blamed. In addition, we are getting more snotty, spoiled, optimistic, demanding, and ignorant about the acceptable level of tolerance in relationships.

Therefore, another objective of a relationship framework is to gradually give us a rational measure of the acceptable level of tolerance. Couples should not depend on their subjective judgment or crooked sense of romanticism to guess the level of reasonable tolerance. Of course, each couple would be the one determining their own level of tolerance. Yet they should also have access to a more realistic standard to avoid gross misperceptions. We must decide whether we prefer relationships with some imperfections to isolation, or vice versa. The question is whether we prefer to live in a fantasy world and dream about a perfect relationship or wish to learn about reducing our expectations. Our options seem to be clear. They are:

- Keep fighting with our partners and ourselves over the irreconcilable issues of relationships in the new era, or live in solitude, while sticking to some rigid perceptions of an ideal relationship.
- Learn to accept the new reality of relationships, reduce our expectations from them, fulfil as much of personal needs outside the relationship, tolerate some inevitable level of relationship hardships, and separate peacefully when it proves unmanageable.

The *ultimate* objective of a relationship framework and this book's discussions is to advocate the second option. This book is less useful to people who prefer the first option. Overall, the purpose of a relationship framework is to discourage the initiation of doomed relationships based on unrealistic expectations. It also intends to stop couples from wasting their lives in torturous relationships if they cannot reduce their expectations. A relationship framework can also help people overcome their fear of getting into relationships and facing its headaches, because ending it would be less hectic. The guidelines of a relationship framework can actually help those couples with unrealistic expectations too, because they get the opportunity of raising them directly at the outset and discussing them.

Another major objective of a relationship framework is to *enable partners relate to each other effectively and efficiently* even when a variety of their personal expectations cannot be fulfilled in their relationship. In that kind of environment, a high standard of behaviour and communication must help partners *relate* somehow with minimal friction and stress. The idea is to develop a self-sustaining mechanism to gauge couples' means of relating to each other on a regular basis.

Chapter Six

Relationship Framework's Components

A progressive and proactive environment is needed to goad couples suddenly see their options more clearly and choose a proper approach for measuring the success of their relationships. It must help them adopt a realistic view of relationship purposes, curb their expectations, and instil a sense of equality, fairness, and teamwork. This environment is what we refer to as a 'relationship framework' throughout this book. We discussed the objectives of this framework in the previous chapter. So, let us discuss its role and components in this chapter. The main goal is to harmonize partners' view of their roles and responsibilities for making their relationship successful or at least minimizing its potential setbacks.

Intuitively, we all imagine that some special factors can guarantee the success of relationships better. We believe that a set of modest standards and principles must define the success of relationships in modern societies, instead of letting couples rely merely on their whims or other people's crude opinions. This implies that we already perceive relationships as an *entity* with specific characteristics. It means 'relationships' must always be viewed as an independent entity free from partners' random judgments and perceptions about love, happiness, and other elusive criteria that only mislead couples. Couples' personalities must not overwhelm their relationships constantly. Accordingly, an important question always boggling partners' minds is, "What factors make a relationship successful or a failure?"

We make statements like, "They have a good relationship; they can relate; or this relationship is doomed, etc." On these occasions, we somehow perceive a 'relationship' as a setting, with particular characteristics and needs. Obviously, the health of any relationship depends on couples' capacities and personalities, including partners' mentality, their ability to relate to one another, their understanding of the relationship needs, their patience, etc. However, we perceive 'relationships' as a state of affairs between partners, which could be good, bad, or whatever, based on measurable factors. For example, if partners argue a lot or are depressed about the way things are going in their personal or joint life, then their relationship is rated low.

Thus, the first step for assessing relationship conflicts is to establish whether the problems are genuine or only the figments of partners' unrealistic expectations, unfulfilled personal needs, or idiosyncrasies. The outcome may not change if partners cannot live together for whatever reasons. However, we would at least know whether the problems are within or outside the acceptable boundaries of a normal relationship. We would know whether those problems are real or imaginary, based on partners' erroneous assumptions or even mental illness in some respect. Many relationships are destroyed nowadays simply because one or both partners underestimate the value of their relationship prematurely. If they had objective criteria to measure the health of their relationship, maybe it could have been saved. They might have realized that they should face the problems realistically rather than running away to find a better relationship, or merely out of spite. The onus must be placed on partners to establish whether their expectations from relationships are normal or misled. It is time to agree that the option of allowing relationship expectations to escalate continuously in line with couples' personal needs is irrational. The present approach would only lead to major socioeconomic suffering around the globe.

The List of Framework Components

A 'Relationship Framework' is a setting for couples to relate and communicate effectively and thus reduce relationship frictions. The best way to explain this framework is to identify and review its components, as laid out below in Table 6.1:

Table 6.1: Components of a Relationship Framework

	Details in
1. Relationships Attribute: **R-entity**	(Chapter Six)
2. Partners' commitment to teamwork	(Chapter Five)
3. Relationship expectations	(Chapter Three)
4. Relationship needs (success factors)	(Chapter Four)
5. Relationship principles—GARP	(Chapter Seven)
6. Relationship models	(Chapter Nine)

Components 2-4 were discussed in the previous chapters. R-entity will be elaborated further at the end of this chapter, while components 5-6 are discussed in detail in Chapters Seven and Nine. Nevertheless, all components are explained briefly below to draw a total picture about their connections.

1. Relationships Attribute: R-entity

Relationships Attribute (or R-entity for simplicity) highlights the fact that relationships must be viewed as an independent entity separate from the partners' identity and needs. R-entity is only a concept to remind couples that *relationship needs are specific and not an extension of their personal needs*. R-entity is the glue that keeps all other components of the relationship framework together. Another way to view R-entity is to consider it both the conscious and conscience of the relationship. It acts like a virtual, fair referee between two independent partners, thus minimizing their need to find mediators or go to marriage counsellors to resolve their conflicts. Together with the other elements of the relationship framework, it forces partners to stay *relatively* objective and thus face much less friction.

R-entity can be viewed as an important third party (the third leg of a tripod) in relationships to keep partners as alert, stable, and objective as possible. Without this third leg the other two (i.e., partners) cannot withstand the pressures of relationships. Developing this type of mentality is difficult, considering our passive and stubborn personalities. Understanding and practicing this mentality in real life sound too illusory and theoretical. However, enough suggestions are included in this book to gradually get an overall feel for R-entity. Anyhow, the aim is to gradually introduce this type of mentality into our relationships and society during the next few decades.

Some more details about R-entity are provided at the end of this chapter due to its importance for relationships.

2. Partners' Commitment to Teamwork

As emphasized throughout this book, especially Chapter Five, a major task of a relationship framework is to develop mechanisms that can **enforce** teamwork in relationships. Yet, without the full commitment of both partners to teamwork, the objectives of the relationship framework cannot materialize. If partners' impatience and Ego defy teamwork, they cannot satisfy the unique needs of relationships and their relationship is in jeopardy.

3. Relationship Expectations

Tables 4.1 and 4.2 (in Chapter Four) provided the lists of valid and invalid (partly traditional and partly superficial) relationship expectations for the present era. Although these two lists are realistic in the author's opinion, they must be routinely reviewed and adjusted according to the specific requirements of future generations. Scholars should monitor social changes and partners' new logical expectations from relationships. The practicality of relationship expectations should be assessed on an ongoing basis. Couples must grasp and adopt both the valid and invalid relationship expectations presented in Tables 4.1 and 4.2. They can then assess them in line with their personal needs and decide on the relationship model that best suits them.

As mentioned in Chapter Four, the expectations listed in Table 4.2 might materialize in some relationships automatically. However, they should be taken as fringe benefits of that particular relationship. The point is that couples must not start a relationship based on invalid expectations, which hardly materialize and last in relationships. It does not mean that their relationship is abnormal when they face the reality. Fulfilling the expectations in Table 4.1 is a major success by itself. With this mindset, partners would not blame each other for unfulfilled expectations or fuss too much about it.

4. Relationship Needs

Relationship needs were listed and discussed at the end of Chapter Four. They were mostly envisioned and developed around the list of valid relationship expectations (Table 4.1). Satisfying these needs enhances the favorability of relationships. These needs actually represent the 'Couples Responsibilities' and 'relationship success factors' too. Of course, this list is not necessarily an ultimate or complete list of relationship needs or success factors for relationships. Nonetheless, the more these relationship needs are satisfied, the more successful a relationship would be.

A more complete list of relationship needs (success factors) should be developed soon after deeper analyses and contributions of scholars. However, in this book, the objective is to go one step further and identify some of the main parameters that can measure the health of relationships objectively. These basic parameters (success factors) would be applicable to the majority of relationships in the new era. This can be achieved by developing a relationship framework that can help couples monitor the state of their relationships regularly and realistically. The framework would help them watch their understanding and handling of the relationship needs. Thus, they would no longer guess the purpose or the health of their relationships arbitrarily based on partners' sloppy interpretations. Instead of guessing (and constantly increasing) their level of expectations from relationships, couples learn to tame their perceptions about the objectives of relationships. They should try to focus only on those limited factors that are important and practical for the success of relationships. At least partners should know that expectations beyond certain limits are bound to cause relationship conflicts and a breakdown. They should know that pressing their personal needs over relationship needs would a recipe for the collapse of their relationship. Therefore, they are aware of the risks they are taking if they insist on following their personal whims instead of staying within the boundaries of the relationship framework.

5. Relationship Principles—GARP

We can no longer pursue a passive approach in our relationships and then suddenly become serious and react when problems are out of control and partners feel defeated. A few decades ago, this reactive approach might have been justifiable when the potential for, and the types of, relationship problems were limited. Nowadays, however, with the overwhelming variety of relationship conflicts, a proactive approach is needed. We now need to foresee and prevent relationship conflicts as much as possible. The new approach must be a preventative one. It should emphasize on educating couples in advance about relationship needs and principles. They should then be expected to monitor their relationships continuously for signs of trouble. In addition, they should be trained to expect separation as a most likely outcome of relationships in the new era anyway.

Accordingly, couples need a list of practical principles (GARP) that can guide their activities and behaviour in their relationships. These guidelines draw certain boundaries that experts agree on as a means of maximizing the health of relationships. They would be regularly studied and revised based on social values and changes. GARP stands for Generally Acceptable Relationship Principles and discussed in detail in the next chapter.

6. Relationship Models

We simply cannot have infinite types of relationship models to fit the infinite types of couples' personalities. Therefore, it makes sense to identify a few models that can accommodate the majority of people as long as they believe in R-entity. Every model provides a particular setting for partners to relate and communicate according to their lifestyle priorities and their capacity to exchange passion and compassion. Relationship models are discussed in Chapter Nine.

Having several relationship models to choose from gives partners a chance to be specific about the kind of lifestyle they wish to share with each other according to their personalities and needs. A particular model makes most sense to each couple. Yet, every model offers an effective way of relating in relationships. By choosing a particular model, couples learn to curb their exaggerated perceptions about the potentials and purposes of relationships. They stop looking for an ideal relationship or criticizing the limited features of some relationship models. As explained in Chapter Nine, couples are encouraged to initially choose Relationship Model 1, which emphasizes on partners' independence and then move up to higher level models as (and if) their relationship matures and their experiences allow.

The above six components of the relationship framework must work together to create a productive atmosphere in relationships and help partners relate actively.

More Details about R-entity

To better grasp R-entity (relationships as an independent entity), let us view it from a different angle as well: In business partnerships, we identify the purpose of the business and the means of prospering it separate from the identity of its owners. Obviously, business partners contribute to, and benefit from, the outcome of the operation. However, the vision and tools for running the business, the strategies to make it flourish, and the means of measuring its performance are all separate from partners' personalities or needs. Partners' personalities and management styles impact the prosperity of their business. However, we do not define the objectives and requirements of a business as the sum of the personal objectives (or needs) of its owners. For a successful business, it must be viewed as an independent entity with specific needs and objectives of its own. Usually partners take special courses to enhance their managerial skills and learn how to plan and perform organizational and business duties. They do not change their personalities because they have to run a business, but learn about the requirements of running a business by viewing it as an important entity. Even for a simple business operation, nowadays partners must learn a lot about planning, budgeting, marketing, negotiating, accounting, decision-making process, performance measurement, etc.

Managing 'relationships' has similar, if not more, demands. Thus, it should be treated as carefully and viewed as an independent entity too. In older societies, the expectations from relationships were not as complex and demanding as they are in the new era. Therefore, developing a new vision and approach to run this important partnership effectively is imperative. A marital partnership is many folds more complex and demanding than any business partnership, because the cost of failure is much higher. The emotional aspect of such failure is horrendous and financial aspects might prove quite substantial, too, in most cases. Therefore, it should be viewed with as much focus and independence as any business venture is viewed. R-entity simply provides the opportunity of bringing a similar level of discipline to the concept we call *relationships*. The objective is to specify its unique needs and operational mechanisms independent from the personal needs of partners. Nowadays, relationships are beginning to resemble a business and too calculating anyhow. Most partners are looking for more things and wealth from their relationships, and they make sure these assets are properly identified and registered, in case the likely separation happens. At the same time, they ask for unlimited compassion (and ELove), too, which usually comes across as hypocritical.

Someone may claim that the emotional aspects of marital relationships make them different from any business partnership. However, the fact that 'relationships' are more emotional than business indeed imposes even more need for care. Relationships need even a more stringent process and mechanism to ensure its success amidst all other social pressures, both structural and emotional ones. Viewing 'relationships' as an independent entity would not undermine its emotional importance. In fact, it would generate better ideas and more time for compassion once the unreasonable needs and expectations of partners are scrapped out of it. The high emotional aspect of relationships indeed places a higher demand for effective communication schemes than it is necessary for organizations. Therefore, couples should stop taking relationships for granted, or ignore the need for special education and awareness for mastering it. Rather, they should start viewing it as a separate entity (R-entity) and focus on its unique needs more tenderly, instead of only pampering their own personal needs and Egos.

Once the concept of R-entity finds universal appreciation, it will serve couples in a substantial way. It prevents partners from focusing on their personal needs selfishly, or even each other's needs. Instead, couples will think mostly about the welfare of *relationships* as a third entity (R-entity) that imposes a set of independent, yet modest, requirements for achieving certain common goals. Accordingly, society will begin to adopt suitable values to promote the relationship needs too. For example, society can begin discouraging too many hours of work out of greed and frown upon egotistical competitions. Family values could find a new perspective. Overall, R-entity says to each partner:

"I don't care what your personal needs are. And you can continue fulfilling your own or each other's needs as effectively as you can. But remember that you must nurture and entertain me regularly, if you're interested in keeping me alive and active. I want good nutrition and your full awareness about my needs. If your Egos, idiosyncrasies, or learning disability prevent you from understanding my needs and rules, then just don't even bother coming close to me. I know I sound arrogant to expect you put my needs ahead of your own and your partners' needs, but that is the only way I can stop you two from getting on each other's nerves and destroying me in the process too."

With this approach, the less (expectations) would contribute more toward keeping a relationship healthy and together. This approach prevents partners from imposing their idiotic expectations on relationships. They understand their roles in keeping R-entity alive, while maintaining their independence and respect too. At the present time, we are only suffocating R-entity with our never-ending personal needs and expectations.

Obviously, every relationship has some unique characteristics based on personal preferences and intelligence of its partners. However, its general characteristics must always fall within R-entity's modest guidelines. This is the same principle that governs in business too. The general needs and processes of business are not dependent upon the type of business or its owners' personalities. Some businesses are complex and huge, and some are small. Yet the general business guidelines apply to all types of businesses. In relationships, then, each partner should honour those basic rules that are necessary for being in a relationship. These rules have nothing to do with personal needs and partners' perceptions about the meaning of relationships. In fact, partners' specific needs and preferences should not contradict the requirements of R-entity. Rather, partners' personal needs should make sense within the context of R-entity. This is because R-entity advocates the independence and individuality of partners. All the logical needs of partners are supported by R-entity. Therefore, when partners' personal needs contradict R-entity, it mostly reflects the irrationality of partners' needs. They might be too artificial or imaginary.

However, the success of a relationship requires partners' ability to grasp and observe R-entity. In some situations, one or both partners may get bored. Or they get fed up with the efforts required to sustain a healthy R-entity. Some people are simply not made to be in relationships, the same way that not everybody has the right temperament to be an entrepreneur. Partners might feel that they are sacrificing too much (by depressing their personal needs) in order to feed R-entity. For example, their excessive need for ELove is left unfulfilled within a relationship framework, which is built around the concept of R-entity. In those situations, when a partner remains demanding, R-entity advocates that partners go their separate ways instead of hurting each other by more demands and nagging.

Obviously, two needy people can always start (or continue) a relationship filled with their exaggerated needs and expectations. As long as they know the risks of doing it outside the norms supported by R-entity, they are welcome to take their chance. They might even succeed in their adventurous journey. Nonetheless, those exceptions are based on partners' freewill and hopefully their full awareness of the associated risks. Knowing the risks of starting a relationship outside the R-entity boundaries might actually keep them conscious and proactive enough about their relationship to make a success out of it despite the odds.

We assume we understand our personal needs and we find them quite justified too. However, how authentic they really are, and how they can satisfy us in the long run, is questionable. Fulfilling them or resisting their temptation remains partners' personal decision, though. The trick is to ensure they make sense in the context of R-entity when we want to be in a relationship. And for this, we must define the requirements of R-entity and develop a mechanism to measure the personal needs of partners against them. The main question for relationships is no longer whether its partners are compatible according to some criteria. Rather, the question is whether partners are equipped (mentally and emotionally) to be in an R-entity driven relationship.

Chapter Seven
Relationship Principles

Some implied *principles* used to help humans manage their relationships, until recently. Whether it was tribal, religious, or cultural norms, some form of ethics and etiquettes prevailed. Those values, ordinarily informal but clear, guided couples to live in some form of harmony. Obviously, those outmoded types of family structures are no longer applicable or useful in new societies. However, the question is whether people can live without some form of norms or principles to keep the families in a relatively coherent and manageable harmony in the new world. The answer in the author's opinion is a resounding NO. Thus, the objective of this book has been to develop a means of returning order and harmony to relationships despite their gloomy prospect nowadays.

Starting perhaps only half a century ago, suddenly all the old relationship principles have gradually eroded along with the advent of so-called progressive societies and mentalities. Those old principles have become obsolete considering the emergence of new lifestyles, women's new role in organizations and society, and other symptoms of human struggle to prove his independence and spirit. Personalities have changed and people have become more complex without any expertise about dealing with one another effectively. Individuals' needs have skyrocketed and their expectations from life and relationships have increased, yet their patience and morality have declined drastically. We have propagated arrogance, extravagance, sexuality, life philosophies, and unlimited artificial needs.

Now we stand at the junction of history. We do not know how to relate to one another emotionally, effectively, and efficiently. Therefore, we suffer from our substandard relationships. Our agony heightens daily because we ignore the current cultural deficiencies. We are unaware of the hazards that the lack of relationship principles has caused. The aggravating hurdles of relationships, mainly due to mounting personal idiosyncrasies, are affecting all of us directly and fiercely while social complexities increase too. Human interactions, at work, at home, or with friends, have become less sincere and manageable in all respects. Family relationships, in particular, have suffered both in terms of child rearing and couples' ability to relate in their relationships. The absence of some kind of principles to guide partners is hindering the job of relating in relationships. Partners' oversensitivity and subjectivity are shortening the longevity of relationships nowadays. In all, there are no Generally Acceptable Relationship Principles (GARP) to guide couples.

GARP is a main component of the relationship framework. It provides detailed principles to guide couples in their efforts to relate to one another. GARP can be developed mainly based on the relationship needs listed at the end of Chapter Four. A replica of GARP is presented at the end of this chapter in Appendix 7-A. It provides a general idea to readers and a ground for further expansion by scholars.

Obviously, relationship problems and their sources are complex. However, the basic cause of all these problems is that we lack GARP to help us understand and respect each other's boundaries according to new social values. A point emphasized in this book is that humans' inherent shortfalls, mainly their Ego, hinder their ability to relate to one another without authoritative guidelines. They do not have the required objectivity to handle their relationships naturally. GARP can fill this gap and gradually turn into some truthful social norms. It can minimize power struggles (domination of one partner) and it can help couples relate more effectively. It must be developed gradually and updated regularly in line with social changes and research to i) reflect human nature and needs, and ii) provide objective guidelines for a harmonious companionship.

The bottom line is that we must be willing to sacrifice in some respects to gain the tranquility of manageable relationships. And we must learn how to tame our Egos to accept and honour GARP. The wedding woes we exchange superficially should be strengthened by GARP. In a sense, GARP is a refined set of etiquettes to help couples get along in their relationships. As shown in Appendix 7-A (a replica of GARP on page 122), GARP merely provides all the points mentioned in this book about Relationship Framework in a simple narrative format.

The following questions require some elaboration and thus tackled in the remainder of this chapter:

1. Can GARP really solve our relationship problems?
2. Is developing GARP feasible?
3. How can GARP be developed and propagated?
4. What a replica of GARP looks like?

Can GARP Solve Our Relationship Problems?

Yes, it can, in at least two ways: 1) By providing a direction for relationships, and 2) by raising partners' objectivity. It would also fulfil a dozen objectives listed below.

List of GARP's Objectives

1. *GARP can help us* **capture and propagate the main features of a successful relationship.** It can show how a relationship may thrive, what it is supposed to achieve, and what we can expect from it. GARP will provide the list of success factors in relationships too, like the ones offered in Chapter Four. Accordingly, GARP replaces the arbitrary (subjective) criteria that couples nowadays use for running their relationships or assessing its viability. This will bring objectivity back into relationships.

2. *GARP can help us* **realize our psychological limitations as human beings.** It can show how our personal limitations cause relationship problems. GARP can enhance our sensitivity toward our partners, reduce our expectations from them, and mitigate our apprehension about the substandard environment of relationships.

3. *GARP can help us* **realize why individuals' psychological defects are not easily repairable.** It will emphasize that we must find the means of circumventing those defects as much as possible instead of criticizing them. Some of the ideas discussed in this book regarding human psychology can be adopted as *principles* and included in GARP. For example, we can agree that, as a plausible principle, 'People can hardly change themselves.' One reason is that for a person to change, he/she must change his/her cognition, which in return requires accessing the depth of his/her unconscious. He/she must draw upon some extraordinary energy and spirituality to become a better human. A principle in GARP may reflect that 'The positive thinking methods, which attempt to give people a power to change themselves and improve their lives, would hardly provide the deep conviction and gradual enlightenment required for change.' Only ongoing meditation and realization, to grasp our Self more tangibly, might help.

4. *GARP can help us* **realize that couple's need for independence cannot and should not be restricted in relationships.** The new models and principles of relationships should be built around one fundamental fact: That majority of people nowadays find the highest social value in personal independence. This is a prevalent perspective after the advent of the women's lib movement and race equality struggles. Despite the inherent perception of dependence in relationships, as well as humans' instinctual need for dependence, our desire for independence is overwhelming every thought and action we engage in nowadays. Therefore, GARP should advocate this general trend that is preoccupying people. But then, for pursuing this basic principle consistently, there is a high demand on people to plan their personal lives as independently as possible, especially in their relationships. This includes maintaining financial independence, while respecting the spirit of cooperation and teamwork in their relationships more than ever.

5. *GARP can help us* **realize that a dysfunctional relationship must be terminated civilly and easily.** To insist on correcting the inherent personality flaws of our partners, or retaliating relentlessly to make them suffer, is futile and childish. Once we believe in GARP's objectives and the other facts discussed throughout this book, we appreciate our partners' helplessness in terms of their personality flaws and perceptions. With this mindset, we might at last realize the futility of our lifelong struggle to either change our partners to suit our needs, or retaliate in order to make them suffer the way they make us suffer. Partners might find GARP, and the idea of treating relationships objectively, beyond their patience or capacity. In that case, they must courageously submit to a friendly separation. Ending unmanageable relationships should be a natural and automatic process.

6. *GARP can help us* **realize that the focus for correcting re-lationship conflicts is not our partner but ourselves.** As stated often in this book, the only way to make relationships work is by having each partner work on his/her own flaws individually and honestly. They must commit themselves to become a better person regardless of its benefits for the relationship. A partner's decision to be a better person and how to pursue this impossible mission is a personal matter and challenge. Partners should not pressure each other to become a better person to save their relationship. It would not work this way. It requires personal conviction, which cannot be forced upon someone. A decision to change lies only in the hands of each partner.

   The goal of self-awareness is to prepare a partner to curb his/her Ego, tolerate relationship flaws better, and accept his/her partner's shortfalls easier, unless the situation deteriorates beyond tolerance.

7. *GARP can help us* **create a means of dealing with our re-lationships without the need to depend on government or religious rules.** The more comprehensive GARP becomes, and the more it is universally accepted by couples, the less people need the government or religious rules to interfere with their relationships. The clarity of GARP should help couples discuss their relationship bottlenecks objectively and judge the possibility of saving it or terminating it. Relationships start based on goodwill and optimism, yet we may get tired of our partner and wish to leave him or her, which is a natural reaction and must be honoured by everybody. Yet, the main cause of separations nowadays is the lack of principles to guide relationships and to measure their health regularly. If GARP can fill this gap, there would be no need to depend on bureaucratic, expensive, and time-consuming processes of governments to resolve our differences and facilitate separation.

8. *GARP can help us* **establish relationship norms that fit the socioeconomic profile of the new era.** It must also remain dynamic and be modified as humanity progresses into more complex environments. All the evidences indicate that life and lifestyles will get horrifically complex for so many reasons. This is true even if we adopt an optimistic viewpoint and imagine that we would not destroy humanity and the Earth altogether within a few centuries. Nonetheless, GARP should fit the requirements of the time. And it must be dynamic and progressive in order to be effective. For example, partners' need for independence is a main theme of the present era. It has been only a few decades since we, especially women, have become adamant about independence. It has now been integrated within all facets of social life, including relationships. Many other psychological developments and structural changes have occurred in society, including our expanding appetite for sexuality, compassion, consumption, and children's prominent role and demands in family life. They all affect the format of GARP, but nothing overwhelms GARP's theme in the 21st century as much as partners' unrelenting demands for identity and independence do. Nobody can say with certainty that in a century or so we will not feel exactly the opposite, i.e., demand dependence more heroically. People may finally realize that for real compassion they need to establish some rules of dependence. Suddenly dependence might become the new reality as much as independence is nowadays. This would actually be a rational progression that the author believes will happen. It would reflect either the humans' ultimate defeat and desperation or a higher level of human maturity, which is a possibility, although so remote.

As discussed before, couples are still not quite aware of the conflict that their prominent demand for individualism has brought about. They are unaware of the scope of conflict that their demand for large levels of both dependence and independence has created in their relationships. They subtly expect relationships to satisfy their need for dependency while they pretend and shout independence publicly. The implicit urge for dependence, while insisting on independence explicitly and noisily, is one of the major hurdles in relationships in the new era. We all must realize that we cannot have it both ways; to eat our cake and have it too.

9. *GARP can help us* **provide the guidelines for couple's teamwork.** GARP must be somewhat proactive in terms of suggesting the basic models and principles of teamwork and negotiating. In fact, GARP must be developed with the intention of enforcing teamwork. Couples need tools to help them deal with a large variety of conflicts in relationships. Instead of suggesting all kinds of untested models or ideas, however, GARP's initial guidelines must remain general and flexible while more precise ones are developed and tested gradually. It would take a few decades before a well-crafted set of guidelines, especially for teamwork, is developed by experts and made available to couples.

10. *GARP can help us* **choose the right relationship model and pinpoint the factors of compatibility between couples in order to minimize mismatches.** Based on their personality and needs, partners can choose the right model of relationship for them by using GARP's guidelines. These guidelines might also pinpoint the areas of potential conflicts between partners according to the relationship model chosen. Instead of looking for compatibility factors, as is the trend presently, GARP may suggest only those principles that can help couples *relate* effectively within the context of their relationship. Preventing mismatches in relationships and pinpointing the areas that conflicts could arise is another objective of GARP. This is different from the task of finding compatible partners. The existing compatibility tests have so far proven inadequate for developing effective relationships.

11. *GARP can help us* **work within a uniform framework to assess our relationships and communicate objectively.** Psychologists and marriage counsellors can communicate amongst themselves according to these guidelines instead of offering a variety of personal or unproven methods. The existing techniques are not focused enough in terms of tackling the roots of relationship problems. Thus, another objective of GARP is to create a uniform framework and language for psychologists and counsellors. Uniformity would not only make the diagnosis and treatment of relationship conflicts easier and transferable amongst experts, but also reduce the level of confusion and frustration for couples when each expert suggests something different and none of them works anyway. Couples are already suffering from their relationship conflicts and they do not need to be confused even more. They need a universally tested system to help them one way or another.

12. *GARP can help us* **view *relationships* as an independent, unique entity (R-entity), which is larger than the sum of the two individuals in it.** R-entity, as a fundamental principle by itself, has to be included in GARP. The idea is to bring objectivity into relationships instead of depending on subjective and unrealistic impressions of couples to define their relationships. Various characteristics of R-entity are listed in GARP for clarity and application. However, other principles listed in GARP would support R-entity as well. R-entity is the nucleus for developing the relationship framework and related concepts. It is the conceptual platform for us to make our relationships thrive.

Once the public grasp the benefits of having plausible objectives and a direction for their relationships, they would feel more willing to stick to some form of principles too. GARP will be an easy-to-read document for the public. It will list the facts and guidelines about relationships according to the social setting of the time. The author believes that people would eventually appreciate the validity and significance of GARP's objectives. Thus, they will find it in their interest to modify their mindsets in order to make their relationships manageable and live in some form of harmony. In all, GARP is intended to become a practical Bible for relationships.

The main purpose of GARP is *to establish a platform for couples to relate emotionally, effectively, and efficiently.* In this sense, GARP will help them adjust their rampant presumptions about themselves and their partners. It will become a point of reference, a defendable social norm, to measure couples' expectations and attitude. It will pinpoint the issues causing misperceptions and marital clashes. GARP will also contain all the information and guidelines for constructing and maintaining the 'relationship framework' and its components.

Is Developing GARP Feasible?

Yes, it is, despite people's major resistance at the outset. Developing new guidelines for relationships is a great challenge in terms of its mechanics. However, getting experts' universal acceptance of its contents is the hardest part. Therefore, the answer to the feasibility of developing GARP remains a reserved yes. The reservation is about the timeframe when most feasible principles are considered 'acceptable' as social norms and included in GARP. The other obvious reservation is the timeframe for the majority of people to develop the right mindset for adopting GARP.

Yet, creating GARP is not an impossible task. It can be easily developed around the relationship success factors listed in Chapter Four—the realistic relationship needs. Let us assume that this is a realistic list, and in line with our social values at the present time. The list must be modified regularly, of course, in order to reflect social changes, while keeping the unrealistic expectations out. Every relationship need listed in

Chapter Four can be expanded into a bunch of principles, which would guide the matter of fulfilling that particular need. The replica of GARP presented at the end of this chapter (Appendix 7-A) is created in this manner. That is, every need Chapter Four is expanded into a bunch of principles in GARP. In addition, the large volume of hypotheses presented in all chapters of this book can be gradually verified and included in GARP to increase couples' understanding about relationships, their hurdles, etc.

All we need for creating GARP is innovative ideas (like the radical solutions in Chapter Eight and other parts of this book) to reassess relationships in the existing social environment. In fact, the main points discussed in this book can be included in different sections of GARP.

We need principles that stir teamwork and curtail the level of relationship frictions. We know the basics already. Individualism and independence have become the dominating themes of the new society. Therefore, we have the platform to build principles around these basic needs of individuals. We have to identify a practical balance between couples' personal needs and the relationship needs in the new era and define those boundaries in GARP. Once we pinpoint the conflicts between personal needs and the relationship needs, we should be able to devise effective principles and then learn to live with our choices in harmony.

Therefore, in the author's opinion, it is feasible to create GARP as soon as we agree that we need it. All this book is hoping to achieve is to spread the seeds for future thoughts. After all, we are all after the same objective: to be happier in our relationships. But again, when we examine the reality, a full-fledged application of GARP may not become a universal concept until the 22nd century. The author is choosing the year 2115 as a reasonable timeframe for GARP being fully developed and finding a universal acceptance. This arbitrary date may appear too optimistic or pessimistic depending on the viewpoints of various groups. The author realizes this fact as well.

How Can GARP Be Developed?

Despite its slow universal acceptance in the immediate future, GARP must be developed and expanded continuously based on trial and error and research findings of scholars. It helps if scholars and interested groups get involved right away. The public should recognize the benefits of GARP and ask for its development. Once a platform is defined and accepted by prominent sociologists, psychologists, and the population at large, modifying and expanding GARP would be an automatic process like all other social processes in progressive societies of the future. We just have to remain optimistic and hope that future societies are given a chance to flourish out of the chaos we have created for ourselves and our children. Ideally, a non-profit foundation can be created to oversee the development and dissemination of GARP.

The success of GARP depends on our conviction about its ability to help relationships. However, the author believes that this task would be somehow imposed upon us, whether we like it or not, sooner or later. We will be forced eventually to do something about the agony of relationships and the lack of principles. We will soon get fed up with our arbitrary assessments of relationships and our emotional decisions about the level of tolerance needed in relationships. Our children will hopefully learn from our mistakes and shattered hopes to find a soul mate. It is just a matter of time and the level of our stubbornness to pursue idealism, instead of accepting the reality.

In terms of propagating GARP, we must simply introduce it at as many public forums and social gatherings as possible. Experts must advocate the objectives of this book. They must find innovative ways of informing the public about the flaws of our existing ways. They must do more empirical research and be more proactive in terms of changing couples' mindsets about relationships.

Despite the major initial resistance, the advantages of GARP will become clear to the public when managing relationships gets totally out of control and couples' frustration cripples society. Liberal and logical individuals begin to join in and adopt GARP in order to test new options for their relationships. They will support the rather radical approaches with open minds. The outcome will eventually encourage sceptical individuals to join the movement, too, in order to mitigate their hardships and loneliness.

Books can help us, too, to comprehend our personality flaws in terms of dealing with others, especially our partners. They must show that animosity, arrogance, and retaliation are unproductive, because such attitude and approach only make it more difficult for people to perceive each other's intentions correctly and react to them humanly. We may also realize that as human beings, with the objective of reaching our deep potentials, we are wasting too much time and energy on the petty problems of relationships. This is absurd and a sin.

It is beyond the scope of this book to explain the mechanisms of developing GARP in detail. However, the principles discussed throughout this book provide enough material to start the process. Let us hope they will prove fruitful as steppingstones for further thoughts and discussions during the next hundred years. Let us join together to do this important task. Meanwhile, a replica of GARP is presented in Appendix 7-A only as an example of ideas that could be included in GARP. It is not meant to be complete or correct. It is prepared mainly by expanding the relationship needs listed at the end of Chapter Four. Eventually, it should be expanded to also include a large number of radical solutions like the ones proposed in Chapter Eight as well as the ideas in the other parts of this book.

GARP's Main Challenge

On the one hand, developing GARP and a new mindset about relationships seems feasible and necessary, although it would take time and patience. Actually, GARP may be the only solution, in the author's opinion, to manage our relationships in a realistic manner. The main challenge is to keep our faith in GARP as a viable solution for our relationship problems.

On the other hand, it might seem rather naïve to assume that companionship needs of individuals, such a complex subject it is, can be solved by any mechanism (e.g., GARP) quickly or at all. Those very same problems and hurdles that prevent us from finding a suitable companion or maintaining a relationship—as discussed throughout this book—would also affect the implementation of new mechanisms largely. Resistance to change would be a major hurdle. Mostly our Egos and conditioned mentality about viewing relationships in certain ways would stop us from changing our attitude.

Overcoming our old habits and urges to entertain GARP or other mechanisms would be difficult, although everybody should logically realize the benefits of adopting a fair and sensible GARP quickly. Accountants have developed Generally Accepted Accounting Principles (GAAP) to guide them in their financial dealing and wheeling. They are supposed to use GAAP to communicate amongst themselves efficiently and ethically. They have accepted GAAP and sworn to observe it. However, they often forget their commitment to GAAP when profit motives supersede their sense of obligation to a higher cause. In our crooked society, even chartered banks and certified investment managers cheat and ignore their obligations. People lose their life savings left and right. We have all kinds of traffic rules and guidelines developed for the safety of the public, but our Ego and temper make us disregard those rules even at the cost of our own lives and the risk of severe punishments. These diseases have inflicted our relationships too.

In fact, in relationships, the complex emotional issues make it even more difficult to maintain a sense of commitment to GARP easily. Nonetheless, GAAP helps accountants a lot and our traffic laws bring major order to our lives despite the drunken idiots who intentionally disobey the laws and kill people. Society is benefiting, nonetheless, from GAAP and traffic laws and all the other general rules we enforce to coordinate our thoughts and actions. It is time to benefit from GARP too. Or, at least, we must begin to envision such a mechanism so that people can benefit from its full potentials in a couple of centuries from now.

GARP might appear doomed at the outset by its attempt to generalize some ideas that touch individuals' emotions and urges. The idea of formulating some principles about relationships by pursuing logical analyses and reasoning sounds absurd already. GARP appears like a bizarre approach in a society where objectivity and logic seem to have lost their meanings. Obviously, both our personal needs and relationship expectations are extremely deep-rooted and emotional. Their psychological effects and power are controlling our mindset and faith. In all, relationships and couples' behaviour are too complex to be studied scientifically so easily. Yet, the idea of introducing GARP appears to be the only option left for society to mend the chaotic state of relationships. Of course, it is clear that applying rules to relationship issues, and human behaviour in general, has its limitations. Accordingly, the development of GARP will be gradual, partially based on trial and error. GARP must remain dynamic and progressive according to new findings and research.

Learning and Adjusting

The process of implementing GARP would require a lot of learning and adjusting. Convincing couples to replace their emotional decision processes with GARP would be difficult.

They should accept the responsibility of observing the needs of their relationships despite their conflicting personal urges and Egos. They must show interest and a mental capacity to function within an objective framework. This would take time and patience. Meanwhile, we should keep our faith in GARP as a viable solution to our relationship problems. Actually, GARP may be the only solution, in the author's opinion, to manage our relationships better.

GARP can also help us recognize the causes of relationship problems. It can also heighten our awareness about our personal flaws and limitations gradually and we may learn how they affect our relationships. GARP can enhance our sensitivity toward our partners, instead of being oversensitive and demanding. It can help us appreciate that our partners' flaws and limitations are crippling them; they are unaware of those flaws or unable to do something about them. GARP can prove instrumental for coping with our complex social settings. It can show how social changes are tainting our personal needs and perceptions about everything. It can identify the factors of success in relationships. At the very least, it can help us understand the role we are expected to play even if we are unwilling or unable to adopt it due to our stubborn personalities. Even this minimal awareness is useful.

Choosing GARP over our personal whims and perceptions would be hard. Lowering our expectations from relationships would feel like an impossible task. Therefore, the main purpose of this book is to emphasize on the need for changing our mentality about relationships and starting to look for the right criteria for their success. We can benefit from this adjustment right away even though the implementation of all the features of a new relationship framework would take many decades. Without our participation and discussions, we would never get the great task of implementing a new relationship framework off the ground. We must believe in thinking differently and acting now too. All couples and society must feel comfortable to adopt GARP and the 'relationship framework.'

We humans have limited ability to listen, let alone learn, about any concept that threatens our crooked convictions and deep-rooted idiosyncrasies. Therefore, believing in GARP would not be an easy task, never mind practicing it. Yet, we must remain hopeful that somehow some of us will benefit from GARP sooner or later. Despite all the foreseeable challenges, we need GARP badly and urgently.

GARP can possibly help a small group of people initially until it is propagated naturally in society after its benefits are proven. Two groups of people may never need or care about GARP. The first group consists of those lucky individuals who somehow find a good companion according to their simple lifestyles and managed expectations. We all envy those blessed couples. At the other extreme, some people are so defective psychologically that no rules or reasons can help them overcome their rampant urges and crooked personalities. Others, those falling between these two extremes, the majority of us, have manageable levels of psychological defects and destructive urges. This majority might eventually appreciate the potential of GARP, despite people's inherent resistance to change.

Overall, it is rather easy and extremely useful to develop a set of simple principles for running our relationships more smoothly and effectively. It is especially important for giving youths a general guideline about the purposes, potentials, and hassles of relationships in the new era.

Appendix 7-A

A Replica of GARP

The principles included in GARP can be grouped and presented in a layman format in the future to make it easy for the general public's understanding. But, for this basic document, the same order of the list of relationship needs in Chapter Three is more or less followed. GARP must be organized in sections, such as the following:

Part I: Structure of GARP
Part II: Relationship Success Factors
Part III: Social Mechanisms Supporting GARP

Part I: Structure of GARP

In this part, the main structure of the 'Relationship Framework' and GARP is explained:

P1. Relationships are perceived as an independent entity, which has specific needs and priorities. This concept is called R-entity for simplicity.

P1.1 Relationship needs are different from partners' needs.

P1.2 R-entity is not driven by partners' personal needs or personality.

P1.3 Relationship needs supersede partners' needs.

P1.4 Relationship needs are developed based on social settings and trends.

P1.5 Relationship needs are dynamic and in line with social changes.

P2. Partners in a relationship are independent financially and emotionally, though partners can agree on a different arrangement at the outset.

P2.1 Individualism and independence are social norms and the locus of relationships in the new era.

P2.2 Individualism and independence set the rules and boundaries for partners to establish their personal expectations.

P2.3 Exceptions to the principle P2.2 are specifically noted in a contract between partners. This refers mostly to financial dependence of partners, but could apply to any other condition deemed necessary for a particular relationship.

P3. Partners understand the Relationship Framework and its components in detail before entering a relationship.

P3.1 The 'Relationship Framework' provides a setting for couples to relate and communicate effectively with minimum frictions.

P3.2 The Relationship Framework has six components as follows:

- R-entity
- Partners' commitment to teamwork
- Relationship expectations
- Relationship needs (success factors)
- Relationship principles—GARP
- Relationship models

P3.3 The components of Relationship Framework are explained in Subsections __ thru __.

P4. Partners follow the guidelines of the Relationship Framework actively.

P5. Partners keep their expectations at the level pinpointed in the table presented in Subsection P5.1.

P5.1 The realistic relationship expectations are:

1. Sex
2. Communication
3. Compassion
4. Companionship
5. Teamwork
6. MLove
7. Friendship
8. Respect- Social acceptance
9. Personal Success

P6. Partners know the repercussions of pushing the expectations in the table presented in Subsection P6.1.

    P6.1   The unrealistic relationship expectations are:

1. Dependence
2. Security
3. SLove
4. ELove
5. Trust
6. Happiness
7. Commitment
8. Longevity

Part II: Relationship Success Factors

In this part, the characteristics of a successful relationship are listed in line with the factors enumerated in Table 4.3. A relationship would be successful if:

P8. Partners are attracted to each other and have good chemistry mentally and physically.

P8. Partners can relate actively and have compatible lifestyles and preferences.

P9. Partners strive for self-awareness to enhance their Self-P and SLove.

P10. Partners know the intensity of, and chaos caused by, misperceptions and try to avoid relationship traps caused by them.

P11. Partners know how everybody's personality is shaped and controlled by forces beyond their control. They understand the flaws of human nature and companionship hurdles.

P12. Partners do not blame each other constantly for their idiosyncrasies.

P13. Partners know how to maintain good communication between them.

P14. Partners enjoy having sex together in line with adequate compassion.

   14.1 Partners do not use sex as a tool for blackmailing, intimidating, or manipulating each other.

P15. Partners are mostly engaged in teamwork to run their family affairs.

P16. Partners are compassionate and know how to show it too.

P17. Partners are good friends. They know the rules of friendship and stick to them.

P18. Partners do not try to change each other or push their lifestyles on each other.

P19. Partners strive sincerely to develop trust between them, but do not make too much fuss about mistrust.

P20. Partners do not try to manipulate, control, or intimidate each other.

P21. Partner respect each other even though they know about and tolerate each other's idiosyncrasies.

P22. Partners are capable of promoting each other's pursuit of social ambitions.

P23. Partners can support each other to pursue their personal goals.

P24. Partners are aware of the Ego, Model, and Self aspects of personality and their roles in their communications. They monitor the positive or negative impacts of these personality aspects on their lives.

P25. Partners know the meanings and implications of ELove, MLove, and SLove in their relationships.

P26. Partners have chosen the right relationship model that best fit their personalities and personal needs.

P27. Partners respect the boundaries set by their relationship model.

P28. Partners are familiar with, and actively follow, GARP —as the main principles of relationships. They use GARP to stay objective in their relationship.

P29. Partners seek mediation and consultation when disagreements arise.

P30. Partners stay honest and maintain their integrity.

P31. Partners are mentally prepared to leave their relationship peacefully when reconciliation is not possible.

P32. Partners do not adhere to retaliation to convince each other about something.

P33. Partners try to be tactful, mature, forgiving, patient and mentally stable.

P34. Partners do not play games with each other.

P35. Partners do not depend on the government or religion to regulate their relationship.

P36. Partners have signed a contract at the beginning of their relationship to govern the financial and other aspects of their relationship, especially for separation.

P37. Partners envision the termination of relationships as a normal expectation in the new era.

P38. Partners believe that termination of relationships should be civil and quick.

P39. Partners measure the state of their relationship regularly and discuss the contentious issues calmly.

Part III: Social Mechanisms Supporting GARP

In this part, all the mechanisms to promote GARP and the 'Relationship Framework' are listed:

P40. Social systems and mechanisms are modified to support and propagate GARP.

P41. Legal systems in particular adjust their processes and laws to minimize its interference in relationships.

P41.1 The adjustments by the legal system and laws are for promoting individuals' independence.

P41.2 The legal system ensures that people understand that they are depending on themselves to protect their own rights in relationships instead of relying on the government to do it for them.

P42. Educational systems teach the relationship framework and its components to the general public, especially to young individuals.

P42.1 The relationship framework, expectations, and needs should be taught at high schools as required courses.

P42.2 The passing grades and requirements for completing relationship courses at high schools are set extremely high and monitored by the Board of Education regularly. The relationship courses are treated most seriously.

Chapter Eight
Radical Solutions

The complexity of relationships is easy to grasp when we study the intricacies of human nature. We might notice how hopelessly helpless we are due to our psychological defects and social corruption. We realize that we are immensely dominated by social values and our personality aspects, e.g., Ego, Model, Self. We are driven by our misperceptions, our conscience and desires, and our needs and deprivations. So, at the end, we face a confusing and complex life even if we knew how to be, and lived as, an independent person.

A relationship gets two times more complex if we add up the complexity of two partners making the relationship. In fact, the complexity of relationships increases beyond the sum of the two partners' idiosyncrasies, as their interactions create many additional levels of resistance and contradictions. In relationships, many new dimensions emerge in partners' lives beyond their personal limits and their knowledge of the self. Even their dormant idiosyncrasies pop out of nowhere. They might even get an urge to kill (themselves and others) due to their deep frustration and helplessness infesting their minds at such an extreme. In all, when couples' Ego and drive for adaptation (Model) interact and incite one another, they introduce a much wider range of potential problems for themselves and other people.

Considering the gloomy prospect of relationships without a 'relationship framework,' the current efforts of marriage counsellors and experts seem unproductive, if not futile altogether. The reason is that, without the proper mindset and knowledge of a reliable relationship framework, partners cannot relate to each other effectively and efficiently. To really help couples, a counsellor or a writer must show them how to relate according to certain guidelines similar to what this book is proposing for a relationship framework. He/she must first explain how couples could relate, for what objectives, and how to reduce their expectations to achieve those goals. These topics should actually be taught in high schools and colleges. Instead, most relationship experts increase couples' expectations from relationships by giving them the impression that they must (and can) rekindle romance to save their relationship through role-playing. However, giving couples false hope about finding their lost loves, or overcoming their mistrusts, cannot help them. It only delays partners' decision about the viability of their relationship. It is rather naïve to believe MLove alone can make couples relate, even if they had the talent and patience to sustain the role-playing requirements of MLove.

Relationship counsellors could instead explain, and work with, the **reality** of relationships in the new era. They can help couples perceive and adopt one of two feasible options: to stay together with lower expectations, or get out of the relationship. Counsellors and authors are trying to help couples make the best of their relationships. Yet, they do not have a uniform method or model to show the requirements of relationships in the new era. They do not agree on a set of principles and a relationship framework for couples to follow.

Obviously, the successful implementation of a relationship framework depends heavily on partners' moods and personalities. It depends on their abilities to manage their Egos and tolerate their partners'. Couples must be talented team players. However, we know that human nature and their conditioned personalities cannot be readily changed. *Managing their own Egos and tolerating their partners'* require a great deal of efforts, awareness, and sacrifice by both partners. Nonetheless, knowing the truth about the reality of relationships in the modern world would help partners choose a viable option for them. It would shake them out of their fantasy world about relationships and realize the naivety of their expectations. This knowledge might help them find a better way of *relating* to their partners and keeping their relationship, if it is worth keeping. They might find a different relationship model to help them relate without a need to separate.

Even a simple admission about people's difficulty to refit their personalities and lower their expectations from life and relationships might motivate partners to ponder their options about a companion more realistically. This basic knowledge could expedite their self-awareness and adaptation process. Meanwhile, they might adopt a flexible mentality to separate civilly when they can no longer relate emotionally, effectively, or efficiently—the 'three-E' factors of relating.

Need for a Fresh Mentality

Relationships would always remain a demanding and confusing aspect of human existence. Accordingly, we must begin to see and accept relationships in a different light, as a temporary union. It takes a lot of courage and effort to prepare ourselves for a possible separation. Even more demanding, we should also learn to become humbler humans and modify our life values. We must build objectivity to assess our relationships realistically and maybe decide to stay in it despite the emotional burdens we endure. Finding manageable mechanisms to relate (in an imperfect environment) and enhancing our tolerance level require a great deal of art and devotion. However, if partners are unwilling or unable to make these efforts and sacrifices, in terms of observing the boundaries of the relationship framework, then the only possible solution is to not marry or separate quickly. Otherwise, we should not expect things to improve and relationships stay manageable only by chance.

Obviously, the option of not having a relationship sounds ridiculous, as seclusion does not fulfil any purpose, at least for the large majority of the population who seeks a companion as a basic need. Both our instincts and culture constantly force us to attend to this need actively. Therefore, we must modify our mindset to bear the pressures of being in a relationship. The particular relationship model that we choose should keep our affairs and communications manageable, while allowing us to deal with our personal needs individually. We either accept an imperfect situation, or do not. Our resistance to choose either of these two logical options—i.e., live it or leave it—only reflects humans' level of stubbornness. We insist on imposing our personal needs on relationships. We wish to force definitions on a concept that is not capable of matching our wild imaginations. In this sense, our imaginary ideals about relationships are bound to give us only agony and hardship. In the existing relationship environment, partners have no definite direction or prospect to look forward to. Thus, something must be done; that *something* is the ultimate objective of a relationship framework. More importantly, we must adopt a new mentality. The required adjustments to couples' mentality have been explained throughout this book. Table 8.1 (in the next page) provides an overall recap of those ideas.

Despite the ongoing struggles in relationships and clues about the futility of our imaginary expectations, sadly most of us do not seem to grasp the root of our relationship problems and just keep increasing our demands. We just continue to torture one another until death do us part. Under this circumstance, the only chance to gain some tranquility and free our spirits is to accept the realistic (and partly sad) options of relationships (i.e., living it or leaving it). It would help to broaden our minds about what relationships can be, what we can expect from them realistically, how and why. We must sense the reality of relationships truly and a lot less selfishly. At the same time, adjustments are also needed in social mechanisms that support family relationships in society.

Table 8.1: Main Adjustments to Couples' Mentality

1. Partners must reduce their expectations from relationships drastically.
2. Partners must know the specific relationship expectations and needs (as listed Tables 4.1, 4.2, and 4.3) before entering relationships. They must also be mentally equipped and willing to observe these relationship needs and expectations.
3. Partners must learn, and be willing, to relate to each other within the boundaries of the relationship framework (Table 5.1). They must identify the relationship model that best fits their needs and personalities (Diagram 9.3).
4. Partners must view relationships as a temporary arrangement, unless they do all the right things (which would be rather unlikely for most people).
5. Partners should be prepared to leave their relationships with open mind, without fuss or retaliation and before they start to hate each other.
6. Partners should view their relationship as an independent entity like a business enterprise. The concept of R-entity.
7. Couples should not look up to the government to resolve their relationship squabbles. Rather, they should depend on their initial contracts that outline their sensible commitments to one another at the outset.
8. Couples should remember that love, ethics, and religion are not reliable mechanisms for authenticating or protecting their relationships. The vows exchanged in those settings are good only for glamorizing our feelings and ceremonies.

Social Trends

To improve the state of relationships, social mechanisms should be revamped to propagate a new mentality in line with the values and lifestyles we crave. So far, society has been dealing only with the symptoms of marriage breakdowns instead of understanding and responding to the underlying problems of relationships in the new era. We are still ignoring the fact that new social values and mechanisms, including legal system, have brought us more agony and disorder. *Overall, for improving partners' ability to relate effectively, the whole relationship environment must be reassessed and redesigned.*

For identifying the needed new social mechanisms, we must first understand the social trends and major changes in lifestyles. They reflect people's mentality regarding their personal needs, which then affect their behaviour in their relationships. The following trends are noticeable in the new era:

1. Social complexities, phony values, egotism, sexuality, and personal needs are rising irrationally. Accordingly, relationships are becoming too complex and difficult to define and tolerate.
2. People's expectations from relationships have risen erratically. They consider relationship needs merely an extension of their personal needs and a means of finding happiness.
3. People's stress level keeps rising due to socioeconomic and career demands as well as relationship conflicts.
4. Nowadays people find their relationships less tolerable than what they had imagined them at the outset.
5. People's inner conflicts and agony keep increasing due to a sense of loneliness and insecurity, whether they have a partner or not.
6. People's needs for both independence and dependence continue to rise. Accordingly, couples find less grounds to relate and work as a team.

7. The rate of relationship failures will continue to climb as people's personal needs and social complexity increase.

8. Each partner considers his/her individuality and independence the most important needs, in and outside of his/her relationship. They consider themselves too important and deserving to live a full and happy life. If relationships hinder these needs in some ways, they always choose their welfare above that of their partner and relationship as a whole. They want out if their high aspirations are hindered.

9. Considering the above facts, couples' commitment to their partners and relationships is at best conditional. They stay in a relationship only if their partner can fulfil their personal needs and keep them happy, while their tolerance level declines fast too.

10. People gauge the wellness of their relationship based on their selfish perceptions and misleading values, because no principles exist nowadays to guide the direction of their relationship or judge its health.

11. People's current approach and attitude fuels the process of social deterioration, while they face more conflicts in relationships and become more impatient too.

12. The above trends are entangled in a vicious cycle that is spinning out of control. Thus, we should expect more of all the above facts in the years to come.

These trends clearly demonstrate the sad fate of our relationships unless we act quickly. They show that we need a new relationship culture to help couples relate actively, or at least passively in a rather productive setting. We should review the existing environment seriously and adjust our mentality. We also need corresponding mechanisms to both encourage and handle the new social mentality. Both people and governments have a major social responsibility to develop a relationship framework and guidelines, but also push for revamping social mechanisms.

Revamping Social Mechanisms

The main adjustments required for social mechanisms are mainly government's responsibility. They are listed in Table 8.2. The concepts in Tables 8.1 and 8.2 correspond almost line by line, and together they present a new perspective for relationships. This connection supports the idea that new mechanisms must fit our emerging mentality.

Mainly governments, educational and legal systems are responsible for developing and propagating the following social mechanism.

Table 8.2: Adjustments to Social Mechanisms

1. Support and propagate the idea of partners' individuality and independence.
2. Support and spread the idea of limiting the government role in relationships.
3. Support and propagate the idea of partners' financial responsibility.
4. Support, and participate in, all kinds of research to enhance the quality of a universal 'relationship framework' and principles that would replace the outmoded guidelines of religion and inefficient laws.
5. Support and teach the details of the 'relationship framework' to the public.
6. Support and propagate the idea of relationships being viewed as an independent entity like a business enterprise. The concept of R-entity.
7. Support the idea of time-bounded relationships in legal channels.

Obviously, achieving everything listed in Tables 8.1 and 8.2 seem too idealistic. Even the very first condition in Table 8.1 (reducing our expectations) is obviously a tough challenge for everybody. Yet, couples would eventually realize that changing their mentality and reducing their expectations is the only way to strengthen their relationships and enrich their personal lives too. Many couples are already making some ultra-radical changes in their mentality, such as accepting open marriage as an option for enduring their relationships. These types of extremes are neither practical nor ethical. They would only make us sicker and more desperate.

The fact that couples go to these extremes in our so-called modern society is actually the best clue that we urgently need some kind of moderate changes in our mindset about relationships. The changes suggested in this chapter will mitigate the need for ultra radical options (e.g., open marriage). We need new mechanisms before other desperate options become an epidemic, just for tolerating our relationships one more day. We need open-minded marriages, not open marriages.

It is a fact that people's real needs are undermined nowadays by the existing socioeconomic mechanisms. For example, while looking for tranquility and peace of mind, people are encouraged to pursue materialistic lifestyles. Our political and economic systems have failed us as miserably as our social systems. All the mechanisms developed within these systems have proven inept or careless, not to mention our leaders, the greedy executives of major institutions, the police, stock exchange, court system, religions, educational systems, and all the rest of them. These mechanisms bring us more stress and depression instead of tranquility. Depending on such an incompetent environment to sort out our relationship mechanisms has proven equally inefficient too. Therefore, we must try to at least minimize our dependence on these systems for sorting out our relationship needs and emotional conundrums.

In the following pages, the items listed in Table 8.2 are reviewed, with the aim of developing plausible social mechanisms and radical solutions.

1. Support and propagate the idea of partners' individuality and independence.

Laws and social mechanisms are supposed to be in line with people's needs. In the last few decades, however, people's personal and relationship needs have skyrocketed without governments having an opportunity to adapt their mechanisms with these new needs. The main hurdle is that people's fast-expanding needs (e.g., for identity and independence) remain ambiguous even to them as they strive relentlessly for that elusive freedom and happiness. Too many misperceptions have infected people's minds and expectations. For example, while couples insist on independence, they still want the government to protect their rights in relationships. This might not come across as a contradiction. However, it is, if we examine its practical implications. First of all, we know that most relationship quarrels and breakdowns nowadays are caused by partners' obsession for individualism and materialism. We have also become too sensitive and get offended quickly when our Ego is bruised even slightly. And we feel too sad and incomplete when our lifestyle is not as perfect as our daydreams. Therefore, we imagine a happier life with a different partner. We are quick to abandon our relationships because we imagine it is not giving us enough independence, sex, or luxury. Yet, we play the role of compromising and modest partners at the time of starting our relationships. We hide our greed and our overzealousness for independence, because they are not such a flattering attributes to brag about. We do not want to put off our partner early on. The point is that if couples did not rely on courts to grant them financial compensation for being in a relationship, their true mentality would have been revealed before entering their relationships and many couples would not have ended up in bad relationships based on trust and goodwill.

Many individuals still view their relationships as a source of financial security and dependence on someone else's struggle for money, while at the same time they emphasize on their independence in relationships. There is definitely some kind of inconsistency in cases like these. For this group at least, the existing rule to split the assets of partners 50/50 (or something like that) after separation is hypocritical. This is only an example of governments' lack of initiative to deal with financial matters of relationships more fairly and realistically. This rule, in the author's opinion, is a major cause of so many separations in the new era. When a partner realizes the amount of money he/she can get by terminating a relationship, or just for punishing his/her crooked partner, he/she simply cannot bypass the opportunity of separating. Therefore, the government is indirectly responsible for a large number of separations. The existing asset distribution mechanism at the time of separation is a silly copout. It has evolved only because courts are not equipped to make a fair assessment of relationship variables including its financial assets. People and governments are careless about the ambiguity and damages (financial and emotional) caused by the existing social mechanisms.

In recent decades, laws and mechanisms have been modified only to deal with the *symptoms* of relationship failures and not the changes in the mentality of couples. Courts have been involved in financial settlements and child-custodies, with ineffective outcomes anyway. However, these legal mechanisms have not addressed the new relationship needs and couples' expectations in new societies. The government has not yet dealt with the changes in people's mindset, which is the cause of all the existing conflicts in relationships. People's mindset, especially at the time of terminating their once precious relationships, is the matter requiring an immediate attention.

Of course, it is hard to find the right social mechanisms when citizens' needs remain cluttered even for themselves. Couples do not know how to go about figuring out their true needs in a society overwhelmed by the ideas of consumerism and phony means of happiness. Many superficial needs have tainted relationships and couples are not scientists to sort them out. They just feel those needs because everybody else around them feels the same needs and pushes the same values in their relationships. Meanwhile, the government is already too busy with so many urgent socioeconomic matters to worry about the real causes of relationship failures. Therefore, it just deals with the symptoms of this social chaos the best it can at a high cost to taxpayers. Governments are just waiting idly by for the course of history to define the relationship needs eventually. In that sense, neither governments nor couples are proactive enough in appreciating and remedying the true problems of relationships.

Generally, couples' need for individualism, not to mention their idiosyncrasies, would not allow them to compromise about their relationship expectations. Their greed makes them competitive and vengeful. These are the facts that couples ignore at the start of a relationship. They are rather careless initially because they are depending on the government to make up for their lack of practicality and sincerity at the outset. Their naivety about the potential niceties of relationships makes them ignore their partners' inherent greediness and rising obsession with independence and self-gratification.

For clarity, now let us look at this picture from the opposite angle: Let us assume that there were no courts to rule on the arguments raised in relationships. Under this circumstance, now suddenly partners realize the need to become more proactive and blunt. They would try to find ways of protecting themselves in case their relationship fails. They would now really exercise their authority as independent individuals and write a *contract* that outlines their expectations. It provides the clear terms of settlement at the time of separation. This approach and mentality have many advantages that will be explained in the upcoming pages. However, the main feature of this approach is that it emphasizes on partners' true independence in setting the parameters of their future life together. It is true independence, because partners would consider all the available information about each other and decide independently whether to start their partnership, and according to what logical terms. Whether their decisions would be perfect or flawed is irrelevant because they, as independent individuals, make those decisions. Of course, couples can always depend on professional advice to prepare the right contract for themselves. Actually, when new mechanisms are in place, so many standard documents would be out there available for couples to use for choosing a proper relationship model and the type of contract that best suits their needs. We are not still talking about the mechanisms at this point. They will be elaborated later. Here we are only trying to examine the concept.

The absence of government to meddle with relationship decisions would strengthen the concept of individualism. It would empower couples' sense of independence when the responsibility of taking care of their personal interests is left to them. They learn to scrutinize on all the potential problems and scenarios, and then plan their needs and expectations in advance. This exercise makes them more careful at the outset and less frustrated at the end when separation becomes imminent. This is what people want and that is what they should get. It is time for governments to treat people like mature, independent citizens instead of a bunch of careless, irresponsible individuals needing protection at all levels even with regard to their emotional issues. This process also would make couples more open and sincere about their needs. They would understand the implications of being independent in their decisions before entering a relationship or leaving it when they cannot tolerate it. They take charge of their own destiny. And those people who are only pretending to be independent can finally abandon their indecision and hypocrisy. They have to learn to become independent, like everybody else, instead of only pretending it with so much noise and rage. Those who prefer (or need) to depend on their partners should make it clear in their contracts.

2. Support and propagate the idea of minimizing the government role in relationships.

In line with the points raised above about the need to support people's urge for individualism and independence, governments should gradually abandon their role in regulating, and ruling about, almost all aspects of relationships. The more they stay out of this affair, the more couples learn to depend on themselves and teamwork to manage the terms of their contracts. They learn cooperation and tolerance. Couples would start to behave like mature, thinking creatures that humans are supposed to be. All possible conflicts arising from relationships should be dealt with according to the contract in place between partners and nothing more.

The absence of government also makes couples more proactive and cautious about their relationships. This new approach would change people's mindset and attitude. There will be less unfit relationships. And couples stay in their relationships longer, because they have initially thought through the stages of their relationships more realistically, especially the heartbreaking ending that a majority of relationships faces nowadays.

In general, partners can resolve their conflicts in five ways through:

    i.   love and trust,
   ii.   logic and compromise,
  iii.   courts,
   iv.   contract,

v. contract plus a combination of the above methods.

Obviously, partners cannot rely on the options (i) and (ii) above to solve their conflicts or finalize their separation. It would be a waste of paper to explain why, though so much of the reasoning can be found in this book already. Therefore, nowadays, couples wait until the relationship is totally damaged and then resort to courts to make all the financial and emotional decisions for them. However, if they had a contract to set the boundaries at the outset, then not only they could resolve their conflicts without hassle, they might indeed take routine actions to avoid conflicts and prolong their relationship. The ideal (most optimistic) method would be option (v), which depends mostly on a contract, but hopefully utilizes partners' love and logic as well. The bottom line is that having a contract is necessary in the new era for couples to manage their relationships. It must become mandatory. That is, governments must begin to minimize their role in mediation and resolving relationship issues.

Many aspects of a relationship (marriage) can be planned for efficiently in a contract. The major role of a contract is to bring total transparency into relationships, especially about the contentious areas that are so prevalent nowadays. Another major benefit of a contract is that the ambiguity of the present situation would be resolved largely. Those people who count on courts' mercy to exploit their spouses would be eliminated from the process of corrupting relationships and ruining the social mentality in general. Standard contract forms can provide a variety of options for couples to choose from and to address their special needs easily. For example, the matter of child custody and support can be agreed upon at the outset by choosing one of maybe two-dozen options that can be predefined in standard contracts. Couples could agree on joint custody or one partner taking the custody of their children after separation, with certain visitation rights.

The matter of child custody and child support could be also linked or not. For example, in one option, the parent taking the custody would be responsible for all or most of the expenses. It might seem reasonable to some couples that the partner having all the joy of raising a kid should pay for its expenses too. However, many other options exist, of course, to choose from based on couples' preferences. The amount of child support would be easy to set up at the outset, too, in case the contract stipulates that one partner should pay child support to the other. The amount of child support could be based on a percentage of the government's child support rate every year, which is set at a reasonable cost of living index. For example, a couple may agree that child support should be at 200% or 80% of the government announced rate for the years subsequent to their separation. For these cases, if the government rate is $500 a month, the partner paying the child support would be paying $1,000 or $400 a month (i.e., 200% or 80% rates respectively). To be honest, the author cannot see why some children should be spoiled more than average children in a modern society. Why should wealth have anything to do with child support? These symptoms are all part of our crooked social values when we assume that some kids should be spoiled more than others because of their parents' wealth. Nonetheless, setting child support at a percentage of the government rate would take care of this matter anyway. Some couples may wish to negotiate at the outset to set the child support at ten or fifty times the government rate, if they really want to. Whatever! The whole point is to be clear about it at the beginning. All of these terms must be stipulated clearly in the initial contract or through future modifications made to the contract only by mutual agreement. No judge should have a right to override these contracts either.

By the way, the concept of couples signing a relationship contract is not new or unromantic. For many centuries, a form of contract has helped couples stipulate their expectations and boundaries according to cultures and religions. Only in the new cultures a preference for ambiguity has found ground, because signing a contract seems unromantic, and also because a group of people benefit from this ambiguity.

The matter of alimony follows the same logic. That is, couples must agree initially whether alimony is necessary at all. With all the push for independence in the new era, the matter of one partner paying alimony to the other sounds hypocritical. Nonetheless, it is possible to include a formula also for alimony, as a percentage of the government rate for a reasonable alimony in line with the cost of living.

The matter of having kids at all and who must accept the role of the supervising parent is becoming somewhat sensitive nowadays too. Even though many couples might use nannies, still the matter of raising children versus following one's career might cause arguments between spouses. One way to settle this issue is to make the partner who insists on having children accept the main role in raising them while the methods and degree of the other partner's involvement are also negotiated in advance and recorded in their marriage contract. Actually, the question of having kids at all would become even more crucial in the future. Partners must decide carefully whether they are prepared and capable of raising children. Sometime in the far future, people might even be given a right to sue their parents for bringing them into this chaotic world or for their way of raising them. This is a good policy for making people more responsible for creating children. Why should children suffer in this crazy world—in dysfunctional families, corrupt societies, and polluted environments? Making children should become a calculated decision by intelligent parents rather than a selfish act to enrich their own lives, or even for socioeconomic purposes of governments. We should think more about the creatures who must face the social chaos and not their parents' happiness or manpower needs.

3. Support and spread the idea of partners' financial responsibility.

The modification of the government role in relationships has the highest impact on the financial independence of partners. Instead of courts deciding about the distribution of assets at the time of separation, partners must agree at the outset, independently and objectively, on a system that fits their expectations. Most relationship quarrels are about financial issues, because partners' demands at the time of separation are significantly different from what they had expected (or expressed) at the outset.

Each relationship has its unique characteristics and must have a specific financial format that best fits its partners' needs at the time of starting the relationship and couples must document everything. Of course, partners can adopt one of the many standard formats suitable for the majority of relationships. The format of contracts is flexible enough to accommodate partners' specific needs when necessary. Nonetheless, every relationship has a financial format, in which partners contribute to the household budget based on their income. This format would accommodate the situation where one partner is not working, temporarily or permanently. However, beyond their contributions to the family budget, partners keep the rest of their income. They might invest it as they wish without the need to report their dealings to their partners. Couples could invest together, too, or share information about their investments. However, the old mechanism that partners should know about, and interfere, with each other's financial affair is no longer valid. Each partner has total independence to make and invest his/her money. Withholding information about one's income or investments would not be considered rude or illegal. Partners' sense of entitlement to know everything does not make sense in an era where everybody advocates independence and equality. The purpose of the contract is to mitigate the effect of the contentious areas of conflict between partners. This fits nicely within the overall objective of the relationship framework.

A contract forces partners to focus on teamwork, the welfare of the family, and setting a proper family budget, which includes all facets of their lives including the mortgage and other long-term financial needs of the family. What each partner does with his/her money—outside their family budget—is his/her business. Partners' attempt to control each other's financial affairs, by constant nagging or through some outmoded methods, would become unnecessary. Most of these finer points would be systematically outlined in the contracts and they would all become standard practices for rational couples.

4. **Support and participate in all kinds of research to enhance the quality of a universal 'relationship framework' and principles that would replace the outmoded guidelines of religions and inefficient laws.**

As much as governments should stop interfering with relationships and conflicts between partners, they should support universities and scholars to refine the relationship framework and GARP. Governments should find ways of controlling consumerism that is encouraging people to overextend themselves financially. They must teach family budgeting and the relationship framework at high schools and colleges very seriously. Governments have a responsibility to protect its citizens against the evils of greed and neediness that are overwhelming all aspects of social life.

In the past, couples depended on religions and cultures to define and regulate relationships. Now that those modes are no longer functional, it is important that governments play a more prominent role in two fronts: **First,** minimize its interference with the *symptoms* of relationship failures. (This would make people more vigilant about the purposes and potentials of relationships and more proactive in terms of finding solutions.) **And second,** promote the guidelines of the 'relationship framework' as a fundamental social structure for couples to follow. Governments should no longer leave the future and health of society to couples' arbitrary approaches, or assume that relationships can thrive without a plausible framework.

5. Support and teach the details of the 'relationship framework' to the public.

Once governments come on board and agree about the need for a framework, they should support its development and propagation in any perceivable way. Most important of all, the relationship framework, models, needs, and mechanisms must be taught in high schools and colleges, with strict rules for passing these mandatory courses. They are more important than sex education.

Maximizing the public's welfare and social health are the main objectives of any government. As such, it has a responsibility to support a type of relationship framework that corresponds with partners' companionship needs most effectively and efficiently. Government should not leave this important task to chance and hope that things would work out nicely on their own in society.

Family budgeting and debt management are integral parts of the 'relationship framework' for keeping families together. Accordingly, both the government and people must remain vigilant about family finances. Nowadays, people seem to have lost their senses about the level of debt they should carry. They are lured into credit shopping, while governments ignore the spread of highly unethical business practices that ruin families and lead to economic instability. People cannot curb their temptations and reduce their expectations. They cannot stop competing with their friends and families in terms of buying a house or other assets before the money for these purchases, as well as their jobs, are secure. Most people do not have the willpower or the financial sense to stay away from *ridiculously prevalent* marketing gimmicks. In all, the level of financial risks that people take does not fit their particular financial situation. And allowing business exploit people's weakness is governments' ultimate disregard for social welfare. Allowing consumerism push couples into depression and separation is a crime. However, governments should also become a lot more conscientious and active in teaching people how to budget and live within their means. Governments' role to push consumerism to strengthen the economy is coming at the cost of family destructions and imminent social catastrophe. Governments must change their own mentality and then teach the reality of life to people instead of allowing the existing financial chaos get even more out of hand.

Another kind of support is to give newlywed couples access to free counselling, especially during the first year. The idea is to monitor their knowledge and practice of GARP. This process can keep them on track and stop unreasonable demands building up. The process is something like giving a learning permit to couples while they are trying to get the hang of their relationships, and before problems spread and taint their relationships. Couples must use the counselling service to learn about choosing a proper relationship model, building their relationships, and preventing problems, so that they spend much less time on problem solving. We need a preventative approach.

In the next chapter, a model for creating a balance between personal needs and the relationship needs is developed. The idea of creating this balance and choosing the right relationship model is discussed in that chapter. Relationship models and success factors are good tools for both relationship planning and contract preparation. They are all topics that should be taught in high schools and during the counselling sessions.

6. Support and propagate the idea of relationships being viewed as an independent entity like a business enterprise—R-entity.

Governments should devise all the necessary mechanisms to focus only on R-entity, as if relationships were a kind of business enterprise. In particular, they should require partners to sign a contract before a marriage certificate is issued. This would facilitate partners' acceptance of the new approach and the implementation of the new social mentality.

Just imagine if business partnerships and corporations were created without contracts and shareholders' equity arrangements at the outset. It would have looked ridiculous and extremely expensive to deal with all the claims that partners and shareholders would have wanted to settle in courts. It would have also looked ridiculous if shareholders or business partners had to go to court to ask for a permission to terminate their businesses or partnerships. The matter of settling relationship issues (especially financial ones) in courts is equally ridiculous the way it is done nowadays, especially considering that more than 60% of people in modern societies would have to go through separation and divorce and have some kinds of claims to settle at that point. Some people have to go through this stressful process more than once. Multiple marriages have become too common already for many people. A contract is a must for starting relationships now.

7. Support the idea of time-bounded relationships in legal channels.

'Longevity' has been a good indicator of a successful relationship. The religious teachings, tradition, and psychological benefits of a stable relationship have had a lot to do with this mentality. Naturally, the longevity of relationships has many advantages if it could be properly mastered. However, three questions must be answered:

a) Are humans instinctively equipped to live together for the length of their long lives (especially with life-expectancy rising so much)?

b) Do partners' personalities and needs support the possibility of living together forever?

c) Do our new social values and settings encourage the longevity of relationships?

(a) **In terms of the role of instincts**, the discussions in Chapter Two, especially 'The Effect of Human Hormones,' provided a resounding answer 'No': Humans are not instinctually equipped to live together permanently. The mere fact that we all have this doubt (i.e., humans' instinctual capacity to be monogamous) answers the question largely too. It means that, at best, we are not sure. In fact, we witness how liberally humans commit adultery left and right these days. They simply cannot tame their sexual desires and adventurous minds. By definition, any instinct is absolutely explicit, permanent, collective, and it requires no deliberation regarding its existence. The monogamy or devotion among some creatures, e.g., crows or penguins, demonstrate the meaning of instinct. Playing those roles is their true nature. They do not have to argue and fight over their gender roles, equality, or infidelity either. They know and accept their roles naturally and they are not eager to change them. Like, for example, a lioness suddenly insisting that it is tired of doing all the killing and that this duty must be shared from now on or that male lions ought to do it. Humans clearly lack these types of instincts and instead keep arguing about their roles, equality, and infidelity. Therefore, the idea of monogamy or devotion must have come as part of social ethics (especially in the older times), or for dealing with our psychological needs and deprivations.

Like most creatures, we humans instinctually prefer our autonomy and sense of adventure, especially sexuality. Let us stop pretending otherwise. Our Ego (and the urge for independence) prevents us from being dependable instinctually. Referring to the discussions about gender differences in other books by this author, it is reasonable to believe that the instinctual differences between men and women in fact goad them to deflect (or even fight off) each other. Of course, this does not mean that they do not fall in love or try to support each other. However, many of these conditions are tentative or the residues of cultural norms and religions. Overall, humans have to make special efforts to get along, especially the opposite sexes.

The urge to experience sex with many partners is in almost all human beings. We put too much emphasis on sex with different partners, somewhat instinctually and partly culturally as a means of finding happiness. Thus, as much as humans' rising craving for sexual freedom seems quite instinctual, it emphasizes the fact that we are not instinctually programmed to live together permanently if we do not like (support) our partners' sexual relations with others.

A cute *relationship* instinct is that men usually try to avoid commitment while women want to lure them into it. Is this a by-product of the women's instinctual need for procreation? Probably not, because women and men of all ages have these urges. Is this really an instinctual urge or only a 'condition' developed because of people's marital experiences throughout the history of mankind? It is hard to say, except for the fact that women seek dependency more naturally, especially during maternity. This condition (men's resistance to commitment) will most likely become even more prevalent in the future as men find it more difficult every day to respond to women's newer demands.

We have accepted the theory of evolution that connects humans to primates and other creatures in general. In the great kingdom of God, the primary role of the male and the female is to reproduce (sexual urge). Their secondary role is to protect one another against adversaries and harsh environments. In particular, the role of the females in protecting and upbringing their offspring is quite prominent. Males are usually less attached to the offspring, and even toward the females, once the initial mating process is complete. Often the females play a major role in cooling off the relationship too, especially after the offspring gets strong. The males obey by keeping their distance or moving away altogether. Humans are seemingly driven by similar instincts, despite the social norms devised to keep them together, focused, and tactful. The evidence for such instincts in humans is not hard to find. We know that:

- Women are more eager to procreate. Their biological clock goads them to get this matter resolved as soon as possible. Women also have a higher urge for maternity. Thus, they are more anxious to find a suitable man and lure him in for the ultimate objective of creating children. Although the women's inherent need for reproduction seems to compete with their career ambitions nowadays, this condition is mostly superficial, as explained below. Deep down, they are more attached to, and protective of, their children than men. Actually, their need for reproduction is more important to them than their urge for independence or career, unlike men. Meanwhile, women's higher urge and urgency for procreation stir their higher need for dependency on men during maternity at least.

- Women show less interest in their husbands when children begin to satiate their emotional needs. Often, children become more important to them than their husbands. Accordingly, their urge and courage for independence grow when the main objective of nature (reproduction) is fulfilled. Of course, if husbands happen to lose their interest or their focus during this confusing process (game), women eventually look for another mate to satisfy their inherent dependency needs and passion.

- Both genders, but particularly men, are lured by other people's charm once their initial attraction to their spouses wears off. Especially, when people age, they crave the company of younger people. They feel vibrant and young when they get the attention of the opposite sex and often believe they can revive their youth by pursuing new adventures, instead of continuing the same life routines with an old, nagging spouse. All of us have this weakness—perhaps a natural way of responding to our psychological need for adventure. The fact that some people do not act upon this natural feeling, due to their sense of ethics, fear, or their integrity, does not change the basic principle about people's natural urge to experience love and sex with someone else other than their spouses.

- People resent monotony and get depressed if new adventures are not instilled in their lives rather regularly. Living with the same partner often becomes too monotonous.

So, people are not mentally (or instinctually) built to tolerate monogamy for many years, especially in a society like ours, which gives so much value to pleasure and making the best use of our lives.

(b) In terms of partners' personal defects, needs, and misperceptions, the possibility of partners tolerating one another for a long time is constantly decreasing as personal stress and defects increase in society. It was shown, mostly in Part I, that, as our personal needs increase, we become more arrogant and develop a sense of entitlement. Accordingly, our Egos prevent us from understanding one another and relating. The trend shows that our personal needs are increasing constantly in the new era and that nowadays we value our independence more than anything else. More independence and emphasis on self-gratification lead to lower longevity of relationships. In some respect, the urge for maternity could be reduced, too, as women put more emphasis on their need for independence, sexuality, and careers.

Overall, people's obsession for pleasure, love, and adventure obviously makes them too restless and thus reduces their sense of commitment in relationships. This is a newly emerged mentality for people that is affecting their perception of life and their relationships. They live longer and want to spend it with people who can give them more pleasure than their existing partners. So they move out of their boring relationships much quicker than it would have probably made sense even a few decades ago.

The kinds of games that couples play nowadays in their relationships for various reasons are also getting more bizarre and destructive every day. The effect of personal idiosyncrasies and superficial needs is making the nature of relationship games too complex and unmanageable for couples. Few people know how to behave and relate to one another naturally in the new world.

(c) **In terms of social settings' impact on relationship longevity,** we must explore the origin of a 'lifelong relationship' ideology, which can be found in religious and morality gestures of many centuries ago. Although the author advocates relationship longevity, the matter must be tackled realistically according to the new rules, which will be explained shortly. Nonetheless, the present preoccupation about relationship longevity goes back to the outmoded mental conditions of old societies. In modern societies, we have new rules, mainly guided by partners' needs for pleasure, individualism, and freedom. Chapters One and Four explain why longevity can no longer be a realistic expectation that couples can bring to their relationships. The old social condition for longevity is against our instinctual propensity and it does not fit our new lifestyles, mentality, and the new requirements of relationships.

As a whole, the assumption that humans can learn to get along has so far proven to be inaccurate. On the contrary, humans are probably worse than most other creatures about relating. Animals at least do not kill their own kinds for such silly reasons that humans do. We do not hesitate to destroy each other ruthlessly. We have killed over hundred million of our kind in the last century alone, by far the largest number in human history. Apparently, the more civilized we supposedly become, the more ferocious and greedier we get. We have the United Nations and we have all these charitable organizations and generous people, but more people are dying every day in wars, from diseases, and from hunger. The so-called civilized countries and their leaders are pursuing their own interests, especially for gathering more wealth and power, regardless of the mayhem they are creating around the world. Heck, the whole sense of democracy has been in a big jam for a long time already.

In addition to the egotistical nature of all humans, male and female seem to have even a harder time to understand each other and get along. People are not made or prepared to be in relationships. Especially nowadays, they are brought up to focus on finding happiness. To them, companionship is only another means of capturing that elusive happiness; or reversely, an obstacle for finding happiness. Nobody knows that the hardships of life and the agonies of relationships are still out there regardless of our naïve expectations and slogans.

Conclusion about Longevity

So, at least for relationships, our social mechanisms should be revolutionized in order to match the new social needs and the characteristics of its citizens, especially their increasing arrogance. How? Well, we could say, let us eliminate the need for a marriage certificate and registration. This way partners can get in and out of their relationships as they wish, like the way nature has meant this basic human urge to be managed. However, since we are social beings in need of some rules and statistics, we must find a compromise. Having a basic social order to register our *marriage contracts* has some advantages too. However, the main point is to make 'marriage contract' a prerequisite for registering all marriages.

A major discussion about the format and conditions of marriage contracts would be necessary in some other place or book. Nevertheless, a marriage contract must specify all the financial and non-financial terms agreed between partners and then specify *a term* (like five or ten or fifteen years) for the relationship too. Setting a specific term for a relationship feels too radical for many people, obviously. However, it has many advantages as listed below in our discussions about reverse psychology. After this initial period, partners may renew the contract for another term, with or without changes to other clauses. Or they could simply allow the contract to expire, in which case their relationship is automatically terminated without a need to burden the court system or cause each other undue stress.

Inserting a term for relationships fits within the new relationship framework quite nicely. It helps partners develop a new mentality that matches their needs for individuality and making decisions with the least amount of hassle and stress. The psychological impact of including a 'term' in our marriage contracts will be tremendous, in the author's opinion. First of all, it sets partners' mindsets properly when they start their relationship. They put more efforts into learning about i) relationship needs in general, ii) the realistic expectations from their relationship based on the terms of their marriage contract, and iii) the relationship model they choose for themselves. They prepare themselves for a relationship that would be frag-

ile (and temporary) unless they show serious interest in keeping it. It would eliminate the artificial needs or motives for
getting into a relationship. And most important of all, partners
respect their partners and their relationship (as R-entity), because at the end of the term they are no longer bound to stay
together. The matter of child custody and all other aspects of
relationships are worked out in the contract as well. Standard
contracts would become available and considered an ordinary
process for everybody to adopt. It would no longer be unromantic to sign a contract—because it would be a prerequisite
for all marriages. The only thing partners must do is to make
proper adjustments to a standard contract, jot down the terms,
and then sign it. And the only thing the government must do,
if this process is supported, is to make sure contracts are prepared as a requirement. Courts would review a few legal cases
that partners might bring against each other regarding the exe-
cution of contract terms.

In addition to a fixed term in contracts for the automatic
annulment of relationships (unless renewed), marriage contracts could also include optional clauses for separation or
terminating a relationship sooner under pre-specified conditions and subject to a prior notice of let us say a few months or
one year by one (or both) partners.

Another radical step that partners should adopt in line with
a time-bounded marriage is to celebrate their relationships at
the end of each successful term instead of doing it so lavishly
at the beginning when there is very little guarantee for partners' ability to relate to one another successfully. Stop wasting
too much effort and money on some event before it is established that partners really deserve to celebrate their ability to
live harmoniously together. It is very likely that they are going
through this whole shenanigan called marriage vainly based
on their naïve image of relationships the way it is misper-
ceived nowadays.

The Magic of Reverse Psychology

The benefits of having a term specified in relationship contracts are substantial. The reverse psychology works perfectly in this case, mostly for prolonging their relationship. Just to mention a few points, it will:

1. Change the whole social mentality about relationships.
2. Guarantee partners' needs for individualism and independence.
3. Satisfy the instinctual urges of humans (for companionship and procreation) without unnecessary formalities.
4. Free partners from feeling trapped.
5. Keep partners hopeful about future and happiness if their present relationship fails.
6. Make partners smarter about life and their relationship decisions.
7. Increase partners' enthusiasm to learn and practice the 'relationship framework' and GARP.
8. Introduce a progressive and proactive mindset for partners.
9. Increase love and cooperation in relationships.
10. Enforce teamwork and give it a more crucial role in relationships.
11. Increase longevity of relationships.
12. Make children's lives less stressful and more predictable.
13. Reduce stress in families and society as a whole.
14. Reduce the sense of possessiveness and jealousy.
15. Reduce the burden on court systems substantially.
16. Eliminate the need for couples to spend outrageous legal fees.
17. Reduce the fear of getting into relationships and facing its hassles.
18. Increase economic productivity and social welfare due to reduced stress and time wasted on relationship wars between partners.

I recall Elizabeth Gilbert's witty and succinct observation in her book, *Committed*. I am quoting it here from memory, which is very close, if not the exact, wording she has used to refer to the hectic environment of relationships in the new era: "I'm surprised that they (governments) are still allowing us to get married."

The point is that we all rather agree that when the society at large faces a major challenge, we hope that some authority (usually the government in democratic societies) steps in to at least play the role of a moderator and induce order before a catastrophe cripples the whole socioeconomic structure. Let us hope we do not have to wait for the boiling point where the government is forced to restrict marriages. Instead, we need the government's and scholar's intervention to bring objectivity back into relationships somehow, because religions and old cultures cannot play that role anymore. Companionship is an immensely important facet of social structure and should not be left unattended for so long.

It will take a rather long time before social mechanisms are in place to accommodate relationships' new needs. However, we can think and behave as if these new values and mechanisms are in place. We can do so by living more independently, writing a marriage contract, and getting out of our marriages civilly, when necessary, without being so vengeful and greedy.

PART III

Relationship Models

Chapter Nine

Balancing Personal and Relationship Needs

A main objective of the relationship framework is to create a balance between partners' personal needs and the general relationship needs. We have developed a large variety of personal needs in recent decades. Many of our needs are instinctual, but we have also created many artificial needs for ourselves due to our drive for consumerism and a sense of entitlement for love, compassion, sex, and material stuff to make our lives supposedly as complete as possible. However, besides making our lives more complex and stressful with our rising needs, we have also made our relationships too difficult to manage. In fact, our personal needs and relationship needs are becoming more conflicting and troublesome every year.

Personal Needs Tree

Humans are driven by a set of growing needs like the ones shown in Diagram 9.1 in the next page. Basic needs, such as food and shelter, are at the bottom of this order (tree). Our needs for social interaction and recognition stand in the middle. And, the higher needs consist of self-esteem and actualization. According to this theory, people move up the needs tree as their lower needs are satisfied.

Order (Tree)

5. Self-actualization/Spirituality

4. Status/Recognition

3. Social

2. Security

1. Shelter & Food

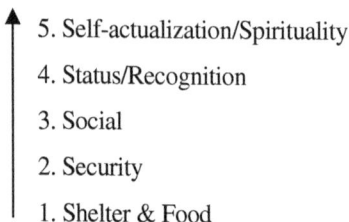

Diagram 9.1: Personal Needs Tree

In this book, our interest about personal needs relates only to couples' interactions and conflicts with relationship needs.

Relationship Needs Tree

The relationship needs (success factors) were listed in Chapter Four. Ideally, couples must satisfy all those needs simultaneously as much as possible. However, in most common relationships, couples are responsible to fulfil some needs with a higher urgency. The goal in this chapter is to rank these needs according to their urgency and importance for the success of relationships. This ranking provides a tentative order of the relationship needs.

An elaborate 'factor analysis' can provide a scientific Relationship Needs ranking. However, a simple 'relationship needs tree' is needed now for the purpose of this book. One way to go about it is to develop a subjective list of ranked success factors for now. For example, the discussions in this book indicate that partners' knowledge of the relationship framework, commitment to certain relationship principles, and teamwork, etc. should get the highest rankings on this list.

Another approach is to develop a 'relationship needs tree' according to the dependency capacity (maturity) of partners. That is, the more partners can depend on each other for support and love, a better rating their relationship gets. Accordingly, we can attach various relationship needs based on the degree of partners' 'dependence' level. Obviously, the more partners wish to depend on each other, the more complex (but also complete) their relationship would become. How well each 'relationship need' is satisfied affects the degree of relationship completeness (success) too.

For simplicity in this book, let us identify five levels of partners' dependency in line with the particular relationship needs as shown in Diagram 9.2 below.

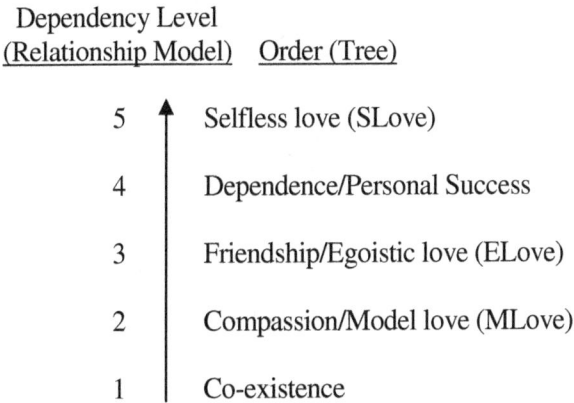

Dependency Level
(Relationship Model)   Order (Tree)

5   Selfless love (SLove)

4   Dependence/Personal Success

3   Friendship/Egoistic love (ELove)

2   Compassion/Model love (MLove)

1   Co-existence

Diagram 9.2: Relationship Needs Tree

The notations SLove, ELove, and MLove shown in the above were defined in Chapter One, which indicate that the higher we climb up the tree, the more sincere couples' level of love would be.

Some of the main characteristics of the Relationship Needs Tree are:

1. The five 'dependency' levels signify the degree of complexity of relationship needs that must be satisfied.
2. The higher we go up the tree, the more dependent partners become on each other. And thus, the more complex relationship needs get.
3. On the other hand, a lower ranking shows partners' admirable capacity to be independent instead of burdening their relationship with their raw demands. In addition, a lower ranking reflects the higher urgency of those preliminary relationship needs that partners must fulfil initially without putting dependency pressures on their relationship until they learn about each other and their relationship's needs, mature, and gradually become more dependent upon each other naturally—and not forcefully from day one.
4. Partners must understand and satisfy the less complex needs of relationships first before they progress to the higher levels of dependency. The problem in relationships nowadays is that couples actually do the opposite. That is, they naively believe that they can start their relationships at the highest level of dependency and impose all their complex needs, including ELove and SLove, upon each other right away.
5. The higher we move up in the above tree, the more solid a relationship gets, because more relationship expectations are satisfied naturally after partners learn about each other, gain more patience to handle their conflicts, and understand the relationship needs and framework. At the upper levels, even the so-called unrealistic expectations (the ones listed in Table 4.2), including selfless love, are satisfied.
6. The higher we move up the tree, the more partners are expected to have balanced their needs for dependence and independence personally and in terms of relating to one another.

7. As a whole, in the lower levels of the tree, partners emphasize on their independence. They move up the hierarchy only when they can demonstrate their genuine interest and maturity to respond to each other's dependency needs as well in a proper manner.

An ironic conclusion from the Relationship Needs tree is that partners need a high degree of maturity to gain even the capacity for grasping the meaning and means of depending on each other. Initially, this conclusion seems rather contrary to the general belief that we need more maturity for being an independent person. However, there is no contradiction here if we think about the matter more deeply. Of course, a high degree of maturity and enlightenment is required to achieve personal independence. However, at the same time, we need even a higher degree of maturity and enlightenment to become selfless enough to accept some sort of mutual dependency to others and allow others to depend on us too.

This is a very fine point that we should ponder for understanding our independency needs and gauging the level of our maturity. A great deal of courage and wisdom is required to ask for, or allow, higher dependencies in our lives, and also fulfil the obligations that go with it in the right way. This is a major fact (and hurdle) in relationships, which is totally lost to couples with the least amount of maturity and wisdom, who also demand a high degree of dependency so selfishly without a sense of the obligations attached to it.

A reason for so much conflict in relationships is that couples do not have a particular relationship model to guide them. Yet, most couples imagine they can start and maintain a relationship at the highest level of the relationship needs tree automatically and fulfil all its complex requirements. It is obvious by now how unreasonable this expectation is. Couples must realize that moving up the relationship needs requires time, patience, and devotion by demonstrating their sincerity and security. They must be really mature in terms of personality, lifestyle, and priorities in order to reach a higher level in the relationship needs tree. This progression is not by partners' desire or choice, but rather an automatic one, as a natural consequence of partners' compatibility, personality, and needs. Therefore, partners should be realistic about the relationship model they choose. They should not demand a high level of dependency until they are sure about their capacity to remain humble and free from Ego. Especially, newlyweds must choose the lowest relationship model at the beginning and hope to move upward according to their actual encounters. In reality, however, they do just the opposite. That is, they assume they are equipped to deal with each other's high dependency needs from the beginning.

Relationship Needs Forest!

It is interesting to study whether and how couples' personal needs coincide with their relationship needs. Diagram 9.3 (in the next page) shows this comparison, with personal needs on the horizontal axis and relationship needs on the vertical axis.

The term 'Relationship Needs Forest' is used only for two reasons: First, to reflect the complexity of the relationship needs when only two trees (personal and relationship need trees) stand side by side and contradict one another too often. Second, to separate the relationships' complex needs in Diagram 9.3 from the basic ones in Diagram 9.2. That is, the pressures of couples' personal needs make their relationship needs even more complicated than could be the case in less hectic relationships. After all, couples' personal needs obscure relationship needs too much, beyond the preliminary needs of a simple and natural relationship. Nowadays, even the basic relationship needs have become too complex, like a dense forest, to understand and satisfy.

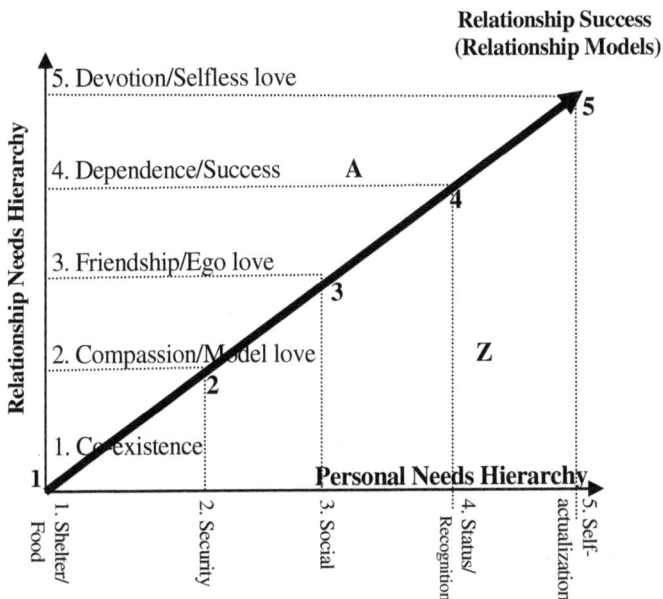

Diagram 9.3: Relationship Needs Forest

Another point about Diagram 9.3 is that partners' relationship needs are depicted as a 'basic need' at the left side of the 'personal needs tree' axis. Although we usually view relationships as a social need, companionship and compassion are extremely important needs nowadays even for a starving, homeless person. Therefore, the vertical axis, the 'relationship needs tree,' is placed at the beginning of the horizontal axis (i.e., personal needs tree), where shelter and food is.

Obviously, humans' need for a companion has found the highest value in modern societies. (This might sound like an odd statement considering the chaotic situation of relationships in the new era. However, the fact that we have so much difficulty finding a companion is actually turning 'relationships' into a more scarce and urgent need.) Anyway, finding a companion is perceived by the majority of us as a basic need—at least in affluent countries where basic needs for food and shelter are not as prominently felt as they were in the older times or as they are felt in poorer countries. Need for a reliable companion has found a profound psychological importance for the majority of people. The unfortunate reality is that the need for compassion is increasing, mostly because people are deprived of it more every day in our hectic social settings. It is also because they have less of it themselves to offer—because arrogance has become a social norm. This point is further explained in Chapter Eleven when the topic of 'Need Urgency' is discussed in some details.

Another correct implication of Diagram 9.3 is that even couples striving for their basic personal needs can possibly build a good relationship, even as high as SLove. Many other interesting points are noted and discussed below.

'Relationship Needs Tree' Interpretation

Diagram 9.3 reveals many points consistent with our daily observations. The most significant interpretations are:

1. 'Companionship' is a basic need according to the discussions in this book (mainly Chapters One and Eleven). It is not merely a social need.
2. Many types of balanced relationships exist, where partners are in agreement about their relationship model, their level of independence, and the level of personal needs that this model normally supports.
3. Personal needs and relationship needs are reconcilable if partners are mature and sincere about their needs and agree on the relationship model that can best fit their personal lifestyle and authentic needs. The points in Diagram 9.3 can fit a variety of personal preferences of couples. The only requirement is for each partner to know exactly what he/she wants, express them in their contract, and then honour his/her words.

4. Five relationship models are defined along the 'relationship success arrow.' These models are explained below.

5. All couples represented by a point in this diagram can relate somehow (passively or actively) to make their relationships work. Relationships that are dysfunctional for some reason normally induce too many conflicts to allow the kind of balance represented by the points in Diagram 9.3.

6. All the points in this diagram represent those cases where partners' expectations (from their relationship) are somewhat fulfilled by a certain relationship model, simply because 1) their personal expectations are realistic, 2) their relationship expectations somewhat coincide with their personal needs, and 3) they know the restrictions of the model they have chosen, and stay within its boundaries.

7. Regardless of the relationship model that partners have chosen, they adhere to the relationship framework and observe GARP.

8. Therefore, contrary to common perception, many types of successful relationships exist as long as partner chose the right relationship model according to their personalities and needs.

9. The highlighted Success Arrow shows the most ideal types of relationships, because partners' personal needs coincide with their relationship needs perfectly. This arrow signifies 'Relationship Success,' as every point on the arrow is a perfect relationship. Partners have created a successful balance in their relationship without sacrificing their personal needs too much or allowing their personal needs affect their relationship.

10. Other points in the diagram (such as points A and Z) are less perfect, but still manageable, relationships. A is obviously a more successful relationship than Z.

11. Point A reflects the case where partners are more successful in their relationship than they are in achieving their personal

needs. They have sacrificed some of their personal needs to improve their relationship.

12. Conversely, point Z reflects that partners have sacrificed some aspects of their relationship in order to pursue their personal goals.

13. Anyway, both points A and Z reflect working relationships, as long as partners continue their teamwork, agree on the relationship model they have chosen, and know how much emphasis they wish to put on personal needs. The relationship contract they have signed and other aspects of the relationship framework would ensure that this agreed balance is maintained. The cases where disagreements exist between partners can be attributed to compatibility issues between partners. The cases explained here are based on the assumption that partners are rather compatible and have agreed on the relationship model.

14. Point A also indicates that these partners are probably not too ambitious. The reason is that although partners can support each other to pursue their personal goals, they are somehow not taking advantage of this opportunity to better themselves. They seem stuck with their personal needs for social acceptance and security, and emphasizing on keeping each other happy and making their relationship successful.

15. Point Z, on the other hand, reflects a relationship where partners' personal needs and ambitions are getting the priority. Therefore, their relationship is not going to higher levels and they cannot depend on each other as much as couple A does. Couple Z is distracted by personal needs such as work, friends, or even spirituality. Therefore, they cannot give enough attention to each other and enhance their friendship. While they are relating somewhat actively, their relationship is only fulfilling their needs for ELove and compassion.

16. The higher we move up the Success Arrow, the more successful (complete) the relationship is, the stronger the bond-

ing of partners is, and the more personal needs of partners are satisfied.

17. The higher levels in the relationship needs tree, e.g., friendship, can better support partners to achieve their personal needs. However, we do not take advantage of this opportunity because we are obsessed with our lower personal needs, such as rivalry and greed. Our Ego prevents us from seeing the larger picture; to cooperate for achieving our higher personal needs. The higher we climb up the relationship needs tree, a higher sense of partners' dependability and maturity is required. Accordingly, people's rising urge for independence means that they should stick to relationship models in the lower levels.

18. In 'co-existence' (relationship model 1), partners can devote themselves totally to achieve their personal needs. This means that even couples who give a high priority to personal needs and individualism can be in manageable relationships. In this particular model, only minimum expectations are placed on partners, just to maintain their relationship according to GARP and partners' initial contract. All partners must do is to make sure they have similar objectives and tempers.

19. Moving up the relationship needs tree is not something that partners can negotiate on. They must be truly mature in terms of personality, lifestyle, and priorities in order to reach a higher level in the relationship needs tree. This progression is not by partners' desire or choice, but rather an automatic one, as a natural consequence of partners' compatibility, personality, and needs.

20. Therefore, partners should be realistic about the relationship model they choose. They should not demand a high level of dependency until they are sure about their capacity to remain humble and free from Ego. Newlyweds must choose the lowest relationship model at the beginning.

Relationship Models

The Success Arrow in Diagram 9.3 also represents relationship models that can work successfully. Table 9.1 below lists the five grids shown in Diagram 9.3. Each grid represents a relationship type (model) according to a level of personal need for independence.

The following discussions highlight these models, but they also supplement the discussions in the next chapter about the mechanism of *relating* within various relationship models. Together, these two sets of descriptions offer a complementary view of relationship models. Yet, all these discussions are merely for providing enough insight about relationship models and getting a sense about the nature of relationship models in general. Details about the characteristic of these models require a separate book.

Table 9.1: Main Relationship Models

Relationship Model (Grid)	Relationship Needs Tree	Personal Needs Tree
1	Co-existence	Food, Shelter, Sex
2	Compassion/MLove	Security
3	Friendship/ELove	Social
4	Dependence/Success	Status, Ambitions
5	Devotion/SLove	Self-actualization

Relationship Model 1: In this type of relationship, partners co-exist in the sense that their obligations toward each other are complete as long as their needs for **food and shelter and sex** are satisfied. This model represents a couple of interesting situations: First, partners have the highest level of freedom to pursue their personal needs as long as a minimum level of relationship need (Co-existence) is satisfied. Partners agree and succeed in co-existing without placing higher demands on each other. In this relationship model, the emphasis is placed on the independence of partners, while they benefit from their partnership in a civilized manner. Therefore, they have the opportunity to develop even their highest personal aspirations without being bound or burdened by their partner's erratic demands. This opportunity begins to deteriorate fast at the middle levels of the relationship tree, as partners place more demands on each other, and they must also balance their needs for independence and dependence more precisely. Thus, as relationship expectations increase, partners' ability to pursue their personal needs is restricted—a commonplace observation. They must give more attention to their partners and their relationship. The higher the expectations from relationships, the more necessary and difficult it gets to balance personal needs with the relationship needs.

The Success Arrow in Diagram 9.3 shows the balance between the relationship needs and personal needs of partners. The intersecting vertical and horizontal lines for each model get longer as we move up the relationship needs tree, which reflects the rising degree of difficulty to create a balance between the relationship needs and personal needs of partners. It also gets harder for partners to reach the required balance between their personal needs for dependence and independence.

The second implication of this relationship model is that even people satisfying only their basic needs (i.e., food and shelter) can reach the highest level in the relationship tree—even Slove—if they are humble and selfless (and are willing to devote themselves totally to their partners instead of pursuing their personal needs and goals).

Relationship Model 2: In this type of relationship, partners are mainly looking for some sense of **security** in their relationship. They expect their partners to show compassion, too, although it may not be quite sincere. The focus on 'security' is often a reflection of one or both partners' psychological or financial insecurity. Partners use some Model and MLove to relate and reflect passion and security. They wisely start their relationship with caution, try to keep certain boundaries, and curb their demands for excessive attention (ELove). Their occasional attempt to fulfil more of their personal needs results in conflicts. In particular, if a partner attends to his/her social needs unilaterally, the other partner feels threatened and arguments erupt. The balance in their relationship becomes shaky and threatened if partners begin to move beyond their comfort zone too often. Therefore, they limit their pursuit of personal needs and stop asking for too much affection beyond MLove.

Relationship Model 3: In this type of relationship, partners relate more constructively with a focus on **friendship**. Thus, they find the strength and motivation to satisfy some of their unrealistic needs such as ELove too. Their friendship gives them a higher capacity for tolerance, teamwork, and making compromises. They support each other to explore their personal needs more actively. They still have free (independent) social interactions without their attitude or actions coming across as threatening for their relationship. They use Model and MLove more effectively to express their emotions to enhance their friendship and the quality of their relationship.

In this relationship model, partners get a chance to fulfil their social needs fully. Still, they might feel some limitations in pursuing their more advanced personal goals without threatening the stability of their relationship. They might find the task of creating the balance between their needs for dependence and independence difficult on some occasions, but overall they have a good grasp of them.

Relationship Model 4: In this type of relationship, partners have proven their maturity to balance their personal needs and the relationship needs. The emphasis is on **supporting** each other to fulfil their personal ambitions. They also balance their personal needs for dependence and independence effectively. A higher sense of dependence on their partners occurs naturally while each partner feels a thorough sense of independence as well. The joy of companionship empowers partners to accomplish even their highest aspirations while maintaining a fulfilling relationship too.

Relationship Model 5: This is the most successful, complex, and complete type of relationship. It empowers partners to experience enlightenment, tranquility, **SLove**, and they relate naturally.

A reason for so much conflict in relationships is that couples do not have a particular relationship model to guide them. Yet, most couples imagine they can start and maintain a relationship at the highest level of the relationship needs tree automatically and fulfil all its complex requirements. It is obvious by now how unreasonable this expectation is.

Partners must have high personal qualities and be aware of their quirks for being in any of the above relationship models. Some mechanisms and 'relating' techniques also help couples succeed in their specific relationship model as partly noted in the next chapter. Discussing those details are beyond the scope of this book, but will be addressed in another book as part of the Love and Relationship series.

The 'relationship needs tree' and the relationship models presented in this book are simple ones. They are offered here only for the purpose of making the discussions in this chapter clear. Yet, these simple models can be expanded and explained in a full-fledged working manual. Couples can use this manual to identify the specific type of relationship that suits them. Instead of the five models suggested in this book, we could possibly come up with a tree that supports probably a dozen relationship models. These relationship models can possibly contain all types of successful relationships that we could reasonably conceive. Couples could use the manual to identify the suitable relationship model for them by matching their personalities to the requirements of various models. The characteristics and requirements of the models would be easy to understand and follow.

Diagram 9.3 can also be expanded to show the balance between personal needs and relationship needs in much more detail. This can further facilitate couples' ability to choose the kind of balance they like to create. Eventually, all these details will be fully explored and available for the lucky couples of the 22nd century. Developing these concepts and models is another type of radical change in social mechanisms that we need, i.e., the topic that was presented in the previous chapter. Meanwhile, we can take small steps, change our mindsets, participate in propagating the new ideas, and learn some of the tricks offered in this book for improving our relationships right away.

Chapter Ten

How to Relate

All the chaos in relationships nowadays disables partners to relate in a meaningful way. Instead, they seem mostly engaged in some kind of a game, or they behave passively around each other to make the best of such a frustrating entrapment. This approach feels like the best strategy to minimize their quarrels and anxiety. Yet, all couples miss the opportunity of at least some minimal level of understanding and communication in their relationships to avoid a full estrangement and the rise of hostility. Partners strive to build a rather productive and active type of relationship if possible at all. They try to avoid appearing aloof or careless, while they gradually develop a particular civilized manner of relating. They hope to keep their relationship under control according to the specific attributes of the relationship model they have adopted. Nevertheless, a special kind of 'relating' erupts in every relationship in line with the particular relationship model that partners choose.

We can classify *relating* into 'active' versus 'passive.' A couple relates actively (or positively) when they can maintain positive emotions, effectiveness, and efficiency in their relationship. The three Es are active. This happens when partners are committed to teamwork and have chosen the relationship model that best fits their personal needs and personality. They know how to live within the parameters of the model too. On the other hand, sometimes, partners have already given up on the possibility of enjoying an ideal relationship together. Therefore, they somehow learn to relate in a passive way instead of going for the separation. The passive way means minimum expectations from their relationship while it still remains manageable. In this case, one or more of the three Es are compromised—partners are passive about the welfare of their relationship. Nevertheless, both types of relationships are acceptable as long as couples observe the realistic relationship expectations listed in Table 4.1. In fact, most relationships nowadays are based on a form of *passive relating,* although partners are not quite conscious about their method of relating.

It is important for partners to know about the way they are 'relating,' if at all, and acknowledge it too. Next, they must find the means of facilitating their communications to increase the effectiveness of their relationship for that type of relating, i.e., active versus passive relating. Some couples can continue to get a lot from their relationships, even though 'passive relating' is not an ideal condition. Realizing the best option for them enhances their awareness to implement its particular requirements effectively. Of course, if one partner insists on relating actively when the other one is happy with passive relating, their relationship gets into trouble. When partners have different perceptions of their relationship, no special model or mechanism is in place and their relationship rolls on an alienation course. Confusing messages between partners frustrate them and expedite the process of alienation. Relationship counsellors can assist couples to follow a particular option (relationship model) and understand its requirements, implications, and outcomes.

How partners relate is a complex process requiring a full book of analyses. Obviously, the more the relationship needs listed in Chapter Four are satisfied, the higher would be the chances of couples *relating* to each other actively. And the higher the relationship model (degree of partners' dependency), the more actively they would be relating.

Of course, relating and communicating are two different things. In some instances, partners might enjoy a rather good communication between them, but still cannot relate because they have different mentalities and lifestyle preferences. And sometimes they can relate, but do not have enough communication skills (or patience) to express themselves. Both situations cause problems. However, 'relating' is often a more important factor for the success of relationships than 'communication.' The reason is that at least partners agree on the relationship model they have chosen and remain truthful to its requirements. The main factors for *relating* are partners' lifestyle preferences, philosophies, priorities, and intelligence. Another important factor is the proximity of their personality aspects (mostly modesty) in their daily lives and interactions, without Ego playing a major role. The higher their modesty, the better partners can relate. A reasonable level of flexibility and patience can also help them express themselves better and thus relate more actively.

We can analyse 'relating,' in terms of the three Es (emotions, effectiveness, and efficiency) for both passive and active modes, as follows:

- **In terms of emotions**, partners' objective is to either enjoy each other's companionship (active relating), or tolerate each other without causing undue emotional distress or setback for one another (passive relating). While active emotions reflect a high degree of love and connectedness, passive emotions reflect partners' understanding of each other, sympathy, and compassion. Knowing about humans' limitations and our partners' helplessness to change enables couples to relate, even though it might not be as active emotionally as they would like it to be.

- **In terms of effectiveness**, partners' objective is to share ideas and agree on the means of pursuing their personal and common goals instead of sabotaging each other or competing with each other. They do this in both cases of 'active' or 'passive' relating, but at different degrees. When they are eagerly supporting each other to achieve their personal goals, they are active. However, when one or both partners are not showing enough interest in the affairs of the other, they still could have an effective relationship, passively. On the other hand, the urge to sabotage or retaliate is common in relationships where partners put down each other to prove their superiority. Generally, in active relating, partners can relate effectively when they work together to establish the *right things* for their relationship and personal life in general. In 'passive' relating, they do not work much together to increase the effectiveness of their relationship, but they also do not sabotage each other or show rivalry.

- **In terms of efficiency**, partners set their goals properly and economically for achieving productive results and satisfying their personal and common goals. Partners relate efficiently when they can work together to do *things right* rather than wasting each other's time and energy. They avoid wasting the emotional and financial resources that support R-entity. The importance of teamwork to maintain civility in both active and passive relationships can never be overestimated.

Some level of compatibility can help couples fulfil the relationship needs listed in Chapter Four better and relate actively. Partners must learn about their compatibility and incompatibility factors that either boost or hinder their relationships. They should also learn about the methods of measuring partners' compatibility in the new era. Those compatibility factors should also determine how successfully a couple is 'relating' in a relationship. Furthermore, they should measure partners' emotional connection as well as their relationship's effectiveness and efficiency. The final score would show the degree of partners' passive or active relating and the suitability of the relationship model they have adopted.

The Meaning of Relationship Models

The 'relationship needs Tree' discussed in the previous chapter shows the types of relationships (models) that couples can choose according to their needs, personalities, and compatibility. For our purpose in this book, only five different relationship models were identified in this basic tree (Diagram 9.3), and explained in Table 9.1. They demonstrate the concept, but eventually a dozen models can be identified in a more elaborate document.

In all, it seems plausible that a dozen relationship models can accommodate the majority of relationships. They enable couples to relate actively or passively, satisfy a good majority of the relationship needs, and induce a relationship environment where the three Es (emotions, effectiveness and efficiency) are present at some degrees.

The following discussions provide further insight on the application of these relationship models for helping partner *relate* as emotionally, effectively, and efficiently as possible.

Relationship Model 1: Co-existence

This is the most basic type of relationship. Partners are familiar with the relationship framework and GARP. They are clear about their *contracted* expectations and stick to them. In this particular model, partners do not have the capacity or interest to fulfil the higher-level needs of relationships, e.g., compassion and ELove. They might have wrong perceptions about each other and their relationship. However, the level of frictions is minimal, because partners adhere to the basic guidelines of GARP and maintain low expectations from their relationship. Nonetheless, the fact that partners are still in this relationship indicates that they have fulfilled some of the realistic expectations listed in Table 4.1, know how to respect each other, and behave civilly according to the relationship framework. In this model, partners are *relating passively*. While all the expectations in Table 4.1 are fulfilled at least at some minimal levels, the emphasis is placed only on certain basic expectations that are *urgently* required, such as sex, independence, communication, and teamwork.

Relationship Model 2: Compassion/MLove

This is the most common type of relationship model that couples try to adopt (and the one that most couples are realistically capable of handling). In this kind of relationship, partners try to respond to some of their partners' need for compassion. They know how to adapt to relationship needs and pressures effectively and express their emotions and needs productively. In the process, they satisfy each other's need for MLove—a sense of being loved. They are still *relating rather passively*, but they know how to maintain their relationship boundaries and not hurt each other's feelings. They try to curb their egoistical urges to force their opinions or needs. The additional expectations satisfied in this model more *urgently* are: social acceptance, compassion, MLove, peace, and personal freedom.

Relationship Model 3: Friendship/ELove

In this kind of relationship, partners are able to show more compassion and relate better. They know better how to satisfy each other's needs. They are able and willing to satisfy some of their partners' (unrealistic) needs in Table 4.2 as well, e.g., ELove. They also know how to be true friends. The strength of their friendship actually helps them respond to some of each other's unrealistic demands for attention and ELove. Although ELove is an unrealistic expectation in relationships, it helps in the development of relationships when it is partially satisfied (through partners' friendship and adaptation). In this model, partners are *relating rather actively*. The additional expectations satisfied in this model more *urgently* are: security, friendship, ELove, and a small dose of commitment.

Relationship Model 4: Dependence/Personal Success

In this kind of relationship, partners are really in harmony with each other. They are *relating actively*. They can truly depend on each other and contribute effectively to each other's personal goals. They know how to support each other compassionately to succeed in their personal pursuits. The additional expectations satisfied in this model more *urgently* are: dependence, personal success, commitment, and longevity.

Relationship Model 5: SLove

This is the highest level of achievement for a relationship. This is the level where partners become true soul mates. It gives partners the opportunity to feel and satisfy their spirituality needs and everything else that one could ideally expect from a relationship. They reach love that is heavenly, selfless, and eternal. In this model, all the expectations in both Tables 4.1 and 4.2 are satisfied. They are totally relating.

Although some or all of the unrealistic expectations of partners (as shown in Table 4.2) can be satisfied by some of the above noted models, those expectations must still reflect partners' authentic needs. The minute partners' expectations are contaminated by their obsessions or erratic demands, the relationship model becomes dysfunctional. This applies to higher-level relationship models even more strictly. Of course, forgiveness, tolerance, fairness, and flexibility to deal with our partners' obsessions and flaws are always helpful in reducing frictions. However, the more authentic partners' needs and demands are, the better would be their chances to move up the 'relationship needs tree.' In all, 'unrealistic expectations' should not imply or be linked with 'unauthentic needs.' The former refers to certain expectations that should not be normally sought by couples under most common conditions (but could be attained at higher levels of the relationships needs tree). Unauthentic needs, on the other hand, refer to such desires and obsessions that are never acceptable in any type of relationship.

Chapter Eleven

Need Urgency

—————— ⟨∞⟩ ——————

Personal needs tree is a scientific principle used in this book to explain many points regarding relationships. A related concept, Need Urgency, can also help us understand couples' damaging behaviour in relationships. Need urgency is widely discussed in scientific journals and books. In this book, however, need urgency is studied only for its effect on the health of relationships. This pertains to couples' peculiar obsessions when they prioritize their personal needs outside Maslow's needs tree. Need urgency is important also for understanding and measuring partners' compatibility issues.

Need Urgency Implications

According to Maslow, people try intuitively to satisfy their basic needs, starting with their need for 'shelter and food,' before moving up to the next higher group (level) of needs. That is, their lower needs are satisfied before concentrating on their higher-level needs. The theory also stipulates that if a person's lower needs are suddenly disrupted, he/she moves down the needs tree again. He/she would have to satisfy those lower needs before climbing back up the tree again.

Yet, the need urgency concept adds another dimension to Maslow's general theorem. It introduces the cases where a person's urgent need disregards the orderly upward or downward focus by a person. A few examples may help:

1. Overachievers usually ignore their lower needs, e.g., social or security, because their need for success is too urgent and important for them. They are so obsessively drawn to self-actualizing endeavours they might stop caring about their social needs, security, or even food. People with this mentality are plenty in society at all levels of needs tree. They sacrifice their lives and basic needs in order to fulfil their unique urges, ideologies, or their spiritual missions on earth.

2. We expect companionship to fall in the category of social needs on Maslow's needs tree. However, in reality, this is not the case, at least in the present social setting. Nowadays, we are too needy for compassion and companionship. On many occasions, even a starving homeless might prefer a companion to food or shelter. This is an example of our psychological and physiological needs competing for attention. A person overwhelmed by love might stop caring about food or security. Some even commit suicide for love or their political ideologies. Often, a person's 'psychological construct' determines the urgency of his/her needs. This could be a permanent condition or a temporary setback. Therefore, the 'need urgency' concept suggests that for many of us being at a certain level of the needs tree is so urgent we can ignore all other needs. This condition is usually referred to as an obsession, but could have other sources too, such as addiction, fanaticism, false pride, etc. Some people crave 'social acceptance' or 'status' more than 'self-actualization' even when they know that their health and happiness depends on achieving some level of tranquility.

3. Ambitious people (or workaholics) actually realize, and suffer from, the lack of enough time to attend to their social life or family. Still they cannot bring themselves to change their priorities. They know they are missing a good slice of life and all the fun out there. They get over-conscious and anxious about their choices. Yet, their ambitions and needs for creativity prevent them from wasting time on anything else.

4. Sometimes, we settle for friends and companions who are not up to our standards or compatible with us. We do this because of our urgent need to socialize instead of waiting for a perfect friend or partner.

5. Even reaching the height of Maslow's needs tree does not guarantee lasting tranquility. For one thing, self-actualizers must create new things regularly to keep the cycle of actualization alive and potent. On some occasions, they might not be happy even though they are at the height of their creativity. So many reasons exist for this. For example, when they are not getting the recognition they think they deserve. In all, satisfying our needs, even self-actualization, would not automatically turn into happiness or freedom from our erratic needs.

Need urgency usually indicates the intensity of a certain need, too, perhaps like an obsession, which might even lead to insanity. For example, a partner might be obsessed with socializing. He/she is happy only when friends or family are around. This need may cause a major conflict, especially when the other partner prefers a quieter lifestyle. People are often too absorbed in their obsessions to consider them excessive or unnatural. Therefore, they argue about the sources of tension in their relationships uselessly. Some people have an obsession for shopping or controlling everything and everyone. Like some kind of addiction, these need urgencies or obsessions can drain the person and people around him/her. Even a simple obsession for cleanliness or tidiness can quickly override love when partners start to get on each other's nerves. And then we keep insisting that love alone can hold our relationships together.

Partners' need urgencies could be short or long term depending on circumstances. It could manifest in terms of mood swings or a complete change of one's lifestyle altogether. Often partners even fall out of love quickly, because of their sudden obsession to pursue a new priority, e.g., to get the university degree they had left incomplete thirty years before. Or a sudden sense of urgency to reclaim one's identity, or attend to one's awakened ambitions. These types of sudden need urgencies ruin the relative balance within a relationship. Partners suddenly face an unfamiliar and intimidating atmosphere and they do not know how to deal with it.

Mood swings are the outcome of need urgencies shifting from one thing to another rather quickly and illogically. Often, they are simply the outcome of a partner's defence mechanism trying to cope with relationship conundrums or to retaliate. Another reason is that couples often get tired of the status quo or get bored with their partners. Therefore, they invent an urgent need to escape boredom and depression. The change is usually radical and drastic, because it must overcome their boredom or irritate their partners. Under these circumstances, partners appear neurotic and irrational to each other. Their relationship remains unbalanced, too, because partners have difficulty grasping the meaning and purpose of each other's erratic needs and moods. They do not know what has caused them, when they would reappear, and how to react to them. This is a prevalent situation considering people's immensely emotional need urgencies nowadays. This kind of relationship atmosphere heightens partners' confusion, misperceptions, and frustration. Most of these need urgencies are psychological and impulsive, and thus hard to deal with.

Need urgency shows people's psychological construct. For some people, their need urgency reflects a deep-rooted obsession that stays with them throughout their lives. This is a static type of need urgency, e.g., obsession for cleanliness or an artist's need for self-actualization. It is a reflection of one's personality. This type of permanent obsessions is at least stable predictable. Partners can learn to either live with these obsessions or get out of the relationship. However, often, need urgencies are the symptoms of partners' mood swings and self-defence. These types of erratic behaviour are more difficult to deal with.

Sometimes, people's need urgencies become critically time-restrained, too, e.g., to pursue one's ambitions or have children before a certain age. In the new era, the urgency to find a better relationship than the existing one is becoming a time-restrained, pressing need too. In particular, when a person is getting old or has left a relationship, he/she suddenly feels an urgent need to find love in a new companion at all cost as soon as possible. The fear of loneliness suddenly makes him/her too anxious. And the need for a companion finds an exceptionally high urgency. He/she employs Model relentlessly and sacrifices many other personal needs to satisfy this urgent need as soon as possible. Sometimes, a person is so desperate he/she looks totally lost and pathetic.

As a whole, another complexity of relationships lies in the fact that people's unique need urgencies (obsessions) usually do not follow any logic. They could go up or down the personal needs tree quickly without any specific order or reason. Time-restrained urgencies (e.g., an urge to be loved again) obviously are quite stressful for the person and people around him/her. Other than lifestyle and personality differences of partners, their unpredictable need urgencies and obsessions often clash create many additional conflicts in relationships.

Need Urgency's Impact on Relationships

The above examples and situations show how our 'need urgencies' distort the principles of Maslow's personal needs hierarchy. A few other general points about the effect of need urgency must also be mentioned briefly here. **First,** as noted before, the need for a companion appears to impose a particular urgency on our lives. All of our 'personal needs' demand our attention at some degree and time. However, the need for a companion seems to be an everlasting and imposing one. It seemingly places the highest level of urgency throughout our lives. In fact, our other personal needs often appear pale and inconsequential compared with our need for a companion. Our emotional needs put the highest psychological demand on our existence. **Thus, finding solutions for our relationship issues has become an urgent matter for modern societies.**

Second, 'need urgencies' of partners impact their compatibility and thus the health of their relationships. This happens when one or both partners remain uncertain about their expectations from their relationship and their true personal needs. When they cannot stir a good balance between their relationship needs and personal needs, they feel a lingering tension, which then hurts their relationship too. Therefore, it is important for partners to convince themselves personally about their real needs and the suitable relationship model for them. Any kind of phony balance would only hurt them personally, as well as their partners. They must be flexible, but not at the cost of sacrificing their natural personal needs or real expectations from a relationship, all for the sake of fitting themselves into a particular relationship model. They should negotiate to find a clear position for themselves on the 'relationship needs tree.' And they must feel truly comfortable with that compromise and the relationship model they have adopted. Since partners' need urgencies impact their compatibility in a major way, **assessing their need urgencies is another important factor**

for measuring couples' compatibility. At the same time, partners should realize that since their need urgencies change, their new attitude could affect their relationships adversely. It could be their own or their partners' need urgencies that might change a seemingly balanced status in their relationship.

Third, assessing partners' need urgencies is an important factor for choosing the right relationship model and measuring their compatibility. Even though couples should have the option of choosing the best relationship model for their type of personality and needs, **partners should start with the simplest relationship model, which is the lowest on the relationship tree–with a low level of dependency on their partner.** They could then try to climb up the tree according to their actual experiences in their relationship and by showing their maturity and personality strengths. The policy to start from the lowest level of the relationship tree should replace our existing mentality to start at the highest level. This would be a substantial social challenge.

Fourth, some of our instinctual needs create sensitive need urgencies in relationships and cause more havoc, as explained below.

The Impact of Instinctual Needs

The impact of our instinctual needs on decision-making and social encounters is enormous as they are the least tameable needs. More importantly, instinctual urges find a high urgency in our personal lives and relationships. The roles that five of these types of needs play in our relationships are particularly quite immense. They are:

- Need for dependence
- Need for independence
- Need for control
- Need for sex
- Need for love

These instinctual needs become too urgent in almost all relationships nowadays. Yet, it is not clear how they fall within the overall 'personal needs tree' of Maslow. In the context of Maslow's model, 'need for control' might be considered a symptom of personal need for security. 'Need for sex' might be seen as a basic physiological need. As explained before, our conflicting needs for dependence and independence actually seem to be impacting our perceptions of all our other needs. 'Need for love' seems to be driven by many other personal needs, as it manifests in terms of ELove, MLove, and SLove. Nonetheless, the real implications of the above instinctual needs are quite complex. More importantly, it is their roles in relationships that are of interest in this book, e.g., when two partners end up using sex as a mechanism for retaliation or manipulating each other. Or in the way individuals' need for independence impacts the whole spectrum of relationships, especially partners' need for compassion and dependence. It appears that these types of instinctual needs have found a true urgency and importance in relationships in the new era. As such, companionship is no longer a 'social need' on Maslow's needs tree. Rather, it is an essential (basic) need as claimed in this book.

Need Setback Hysteria

Maslow's 'personal needs tree' implies that people go about satisfying their needs in a civilized, orderly manner. They are content with the level of personal needs they have satisfied so far, while looking forward to the next level on the tree with patience and objectivity. It is assumed that people are rational and set their expectations according to their abilities and efforts. Obviously, moving up the personal needs tree and satisfying a higher-level need is not easy. Therefore, traditionally and logically, we do not expect people to torture themselves mentally when their higher needs are not yet satisfied. These days, however, people are excessively sensitive about achieving some high imaginary goals that they feel entitled to.

Thus, the atmosphere for need fulfilment is no longer calm and logical. In particular, with all the hoopla in society nowadays for getting rich and famous quickly, the price of not satisfying personal needs has grown too high. Everybody has become overambitious nowadays. Society pushes the idea that everybody can become whoever they want to be and have everything they wish if they just put their minds into it. So, people have become too obsessive with their goals and needs. Everybody is looking for a shortcut to have more things with less work, and to get a lot of sympathy when they are too arrogant themselves. Positive thinking and the idea that everybody can achieve any goal have screwed up people's minds, too. They set unrealistic goals for themselves and treat them as legitimate needs.

The need to prove one's individuality is further pushing people to set fanciful goals for themselves, nowadays. They are hoping to make their so-called individuality manifest through fame, wealth, and recognition. Their needs for identity and success have combined and turned into an epidemic obsession for many people. They perceive all kinds of fantasies, especially for fame and wealth, as their imperative (basic) needs. In all, people just keep creating more artificial needs for themselves every year. To make the matter worse, many people see these fantasies as 'urgent needs' that should take precedence over many other normal life objectives.

Since a large portion of people cannot achieve their exaggerated plans and whims, they feel frustrated and unappreciated. They take their failures too deeply to heart. They feel incomplete, a total failure, and unworthy. Both at the personal level and in relationships, the unattained goals are envisioned as catastrophes and shameful. Simple matters that were traditionally considered inconsequential for personal welfare or the health of relationships have nowadays become a source of major frustration and hysteria. People's reactions are sometimes too drastic. They store deep inner hurts and hostility. They get hysterical. They might even show signs of insanity when a simple need remains unfulfilled. Their oversensitivity regarding their unfulfilled needs is too drastic nowadays. Accordingly, the level of psychological insecurity, frustration, and anger in society is increasing because of people's rising inner conflicts.

Overall, the kind of graceful contentment and orderly growth of personal needs, as is somehow suggested by Maslow's personal needs tree, is no longer prevalent. On the contrary, we witness people's major hysteria for not succeeding to climb up the personal needs tree quickly enough. The author likes to refer to this emerging epidemic as Need Setback Hysteria—NSH. Our need urgencies and obsessions make the matter of NSH even more troublesome.

NSH is particularly evident and harmful in relationships, because couples start with high expectations. They dream about so many of their desires becoming magically fulfilled through their magnificent relationships, by their faithful partners' devotion. When they face the reality and their partners' humanistic inability to respond to their high expectations, they react hysterically and make life miserable for themselves and their partners. It also happens when couples keep imagining and pushing for relationship models beyond their mental ability. Sometimes, they are imagining some kind of a relationship arrangement that cannot fit within any of the reasonable models presented in this book anyway.

Nonetheless, while couples' seemingly urgent (fanciful) needs (NU) are increasing constantly, their hysteria (NSH) and frustration have aggravated personal stress level and causing more chaos in society.

Epilogue

We all have felt the daunting complexity of relationships in the new era. The relationship concepts discussed in this book and the suggestions for radical remedies also provide a good perspective of the chaos and our sufferings. Accordingly, readers may now find an incentive to explore their relationships a bit more methodically and patiently. They can read the other books in these series to get even more insight about the depth of relationship conundrums. They, especially scholars, may also contact the author to provide their feedback and perhaps state some major clarifications if they wish.

Obviously, making all the mental adjustments suggested for improving our relationships and agreeing with the radical solutions would not be easy for any of us. However, if we really wish to have an effective relationship, we should get serious and maybe even read this book again to ponder the points more deeply this time to realize that:

1. Relationships have very specific needs of their own, which are different from the personal needs of couples.
2. Acknowledging and satisfying these needs diligently are necessary for keeping partners alert and objective and thus improving the health of their relationship. These needs were listed at the end of Chapter Four.
3. Relationships are intended to fulfil certain limited objectives for couples. However, we have lost our sense about

these objectives and instead placed a lot of demand on our relationships. We have created many shallow ideals for ourselves based on our naive urges for love and happiness in relationships. The real objectives of relationships were explained in the first five chapters, in particular.

4. It is imperative that some form of objectivity and order be brought back into relationships.

5. Relationships should be run according to some meaningful principles, like the ones suggested in Chapter Seven.

6. The old principles and cultures have been eradicated in recent decades and now no guidelines exist to help couples.

7. It is necessary for couples to revamp their mentality vastly in order to grasp the capacity of relationships and cope with its limitations.

8. It is possible for couples to *relate* in our so-called modern relationships in some active or passive ways and still fulfil relationships objectives.

9. Certain relationship models exist that can help couples relate effectively, efficiently, and emotionally.

10. All the above steps and ideas must be viewed together and adopted as a 'Relationship Framework' for understanding and monitoring our relationships.

We all crave a reliable, passionate, and mature companion to make our lives complete or at least bearable. However, hardly anybody appreciates that without satisfying relationships' specific needs and adopting a proper relationship model, partners cannot relate effectively. Without any proper mindset or training about the reality of relationships, nowadays, we lose our soul mates even if we are lucky to find them in the first place. All along, the best we seem able do is to look for some signs of compatibility as a factor for making our relationships successful. Even then, we try to find an ideal or so-called compatible partner according to our fantasies and misleading social norms. The present methods of measuring compatibility

cannot handle relationship needs and conundrums, anyway. Even measuring some level of couples' compatibility is still in its very crude state. Thus, couples would continue to fail, even despite their supposed compatibilities, because they do not understand the basics of a relationship framework and do not observe certain guidelines for maintaining a relationship.

Obviously, compatibility improves partners' chances of communicating and relating to each other. Sharing certain values and having compatible mentalities could bring some objectivity into couples' relationships. In reality, however, even this basic tool for introducing some harmony into relationships is constantly sabotaged by partners. We not only do not know how to measure compatibility, but also ignore the signs of incompatibility when they are clearly in front of us. For example, when we are in love or need a companion urgently, we ignore all the potential hassles of incompatibility and relationships in general. It seems as if some evil forces are at work to make us choose the wrong partners for ourselves. Sometimes, we go out of our ways to ignore compatible partners in favour of incompatible ones. Sometimes, we prefer jerks because they seem to challenge us. This attitude feels most reasonable to us, too, due to the effects of personal insecurities and social pressures that make us jump into relationships prematurely. The initial chemistry that partners feel toward each other often obscures their objectivity. And quite often, we do not get the opportunity to be choosy. When someone shows compassion and love, we stop worrying about the consequences of gross incompatibility. This is true especially since the hassles of relationships are not felt until we get involved in one. Or we always believe that the next partner and the next relationship would be different, i.e., it would be manageable and nice!

Based on limited (unscientific) findings, the author has developed a cynical hypothesis that explains many of relationship problems. That is, the author believes that people usually feel chemistry toward individuals whom they are not compatible with in any justifiable measure (if we used the relationship success criteria suggested in this book). The hypothesis also stipulates the opposite: Compatible individuals normally feel little or no chemistry toward one another. Still the latter group has a better chance of managing a good relationship for themselves compared with the first group, i.e., incompatible lovers.

Nevertheless, we do no benefit even from the limited value of compatibility assessment. Instead, we depend mostly on our intuition, chemistry, and arbitrary values that society and parents have injected into our minds about relationships' success factors. Sometime in the far future, people may finally find access to reliable compatibility tests to assess where they stand and what kind of a relationship, according to what model, they might be able to build together.

In a group therapy session, a dozen divorced men and women mentioned the following main reason for choosing their ex-spouses. The answers are quite informative.

- Mother/father figure
- Out of pity, I felt sorry for her/him
- Lifestyle change
- To stabilize my life
- To have a home
- I loved him/her (the most popular answer)

Obviously, when the initial purpose of a relationship is not valid or solid, the chances of bringing objectivity into it would be slim. After a while, couples realize their mistakes and begin to resent their partners and themselves for being dragged into a relationship incapable of satisfying their needs (which are superficial most often anyway). Some other reasons for couples choosing the wrong partners are: physical attraction, lust, age, social/family pressures, psychological dysfunction, misperceptions, ELove, obsessions, material issues, insecurity, lack of meaningful criteria to use, loneliness.